The Progressive Era and World War I

★ ★ ★ ★ THE MAKING OF AMERICA ★ ★ ★ ★

The Progressive Era *and* World War I

Tanya Lee Stone

**RAINTREE
STECK-VAUGHN
PUBLISHERS**

A Harcourt Company

Austin · New York
www.steck-vaughn.com

For my Dad, My Buddy

Published by Raintree Steck-Vaughn Publishers, an imprint of Steck-Vaughn Company

Developed by Discovery Books
Editor: Sabrina Crewe
Designer: Sabine Beaupré
Maps: Stefan Chabluk

Raintree Steck-Vaughn Publishers Staff
Publishing Director: Walter Kossmann
Art Director: Max Brinkmann
Editor: Shirley Shalit

Library of Congress Cataloging-in-Publication Data
Stone, Tanya Lee
  The progressive era and World War I / Tanya Lee Stone.
    p. cm. -- (The Making of America)
  Includes bibliographical references and index.
  ISBN 0-8172-5709-8
  1. United States--History--1865-1921--Juvenile literature. 2. United States--
Social conditions--1865-1918--Juvenile literature. 3. United States--Politics and
government--1865-1933--Juvenile literature. 4. Progressivism (United States
politics)--Juvenile literature. 5. World War, 1914-1918--United States--Juvenile
literature. [1. World War, 1914-1918--United States. 2. United States--History--
1865-1921.] I. Title. II. Making of America (Austin, Tex.)

E661 .S87 2001
973.91--dc21
                                                            00-059135

Printed and bound in the United States of America
1 2 3 4 5 6 7 8 9 0 IP 04 03 02 01 00

Acknowledgments
Cover The Granger Collection; pp. 6, 8 Corbis; pp. 10, 12 The Granger Collection; pp. 14, 22, 23, 24 Corbis;
p. 25 The Granger Collection; pp. 27, 28, 32 Corbis; p. 35 The Granger Collection; pp. 36, 37, 38 Corbis;
p. 39 The Granger Collection; pp. 40, 41, 42, 43, 48, 49, 50, 52 Corbis; pp. 54, 59 The Granger Collection;
pp. 60, 62, 65, 67, 69, 70, 71 Corbis; p. 72 The Granger Collection; pp. 73, 74, 76, 77 Corbis; p. 80 The Granger
Collection; p. 81 Corbis; p. 82 The Granger Collection; p. 84 Corbis.

Cover illustration: This photograph shows a group of suffragettes parading through Washington, D.C., in 1913. Suffragettes campaigned in the 1800s and early 1900s to gain the right to vote for American women.

Contents

Introduction

The Progressive Era was a time in American history that began in the 1890s and lasted until America entered World War I in 1917. The rapid growth in industry and population in the late nineteenth century had brought with it city slums crowded with poverty-stricken immigrants, terrible working conditions for factory and other workers, and politicians who sided with society's most powerful members. During the late 1800s, a group of businessmen had begun to make their fortunes in industry and the railroads. Men such as J. P. Morgan, John D. Rockefeller, and Andrew Carnegie grew incredibly wealthy and wielded immense power. They controlled a vast number of jobs.

Americans responded to this situation in various ways and, during the Progressive Era, many different kinds of reform took place. Labor leaders emerged among the poor, working population, forming unions to fight for better wages and conditions in the workplace. Some Americans, known as progressive reformers, tried to improve social conditions, both to help those less fortunate than themselves and to fight what they saw as moral wrongs in American society. Journalists exposed the actions of corrupt politicians, and women fought for the right to vote.

As the early twentieth century brought social issues to the forefront in America, other problems were unfolding in several European nations. By 1914, Europe was at war, and the United States had to decide what its role would be in the international conflict of World War I.

This parade of unemployed men in 1909 called attention to several of the problems in the United States at the time. During the early 1900s, in the period known as the Progressive Era, Americans protested against poverty, homelessness, discrimination, and the lack of decent employment.

Growth Brings Problems

At the start of the twentieth century, many Americans were optimistic about the future. Incomes were steady and prices were low. Farmers were making a living and trade was good in the industrial and business worlds.

American Cities Swell

The United States was undergoing a rapid transformation and there was no better evidence of this than in the cities. In 1880, the rural proportion of the population was 71 percent, but by 1920 that figure had dropped to 48 percent. By 1900, three major cities—Philadelphia, Chicago, and New York—all had populations of more than 1 million. Other American cities were also growing fast.

Americans were migrating from the country to the city, but immigration from other countries also brought about a large population boom in urban areas. In 1900, nearly 500,000 immigrants entered the nation, the large majority of them flocking to cities in search of employment. Within a decade, nearly 10 million more immigrants had entered. And between 1910 and 1920, another 6 million would make their homes in the United States. Immigrants not only increased the American population, but also brought new ways of regarding government, different languages, and thought-provoking ideas.

As cities grew, so did the need for modern transportation. In 1898, the areas that surrounded New York City became part of Greater New York, and new ways of connecting the small island of Manhattan with the outlying boroughs were devised. The Brooklyn Bridge had already opened in 1883, and three more bridges were added between 1903 and 1910. On February 2, 1913, Grand Central Station, at the time the world's largest train station, welcomed the first subway trains arriving through the new underground tunnels.

The Need for Reform

Widespread poverty was a serious problem in a nation that was supposedly enjoying a prosperous economy. A large section of the population, the working poor, was not making enough money for the basic needs of food and shelter. By the early 1900s, nearly 10 million of America's 76 million people were living in poverty In addition, an estimated 1.5 million workers were under the age of 16.

At the turn of the century, it was normal for poor children to work to help their families survive financially. Child labor angered many people, because children as young as eight were working 12-hour days. They were suffering from both exhaustion and a loss of their childhood. One woman, Mary Harris "Mother" Jones, was an important campaigner against child labor. She fought successfully for new laws to keep children in school and out of the workplace. Meanwhile, other reformers campaigned for more schools for these children.

Children working in factories and mills were a common sight in 1909, when this photograph was taken. Children from poor families had to work and therefore they missed out on an education. This meant they were probably destined for a future of unskilled labor and poverty.

Children were not alone in their suffering. The clothing industry was notorious for its poor treatment of workers, particularly in the many "sweatshops," small garment workshops where immigrants toiled under terrible conditions.

Reforms in Native American Society

While reformers worked among white, urban society in the Progressive Era, little was done to help Native Americans, some of the poorest people in the nation. Until the 1880s, United States policy toward Indians had been simply to confine tribal people to reservations as more and more white settlers moved onto what had once been Native American homelands. In 1887, the Dawes Act reversed this policy by breaking up the reservations into allotments to be occupied and farmed by single families. The aim was to make Native Americans live like white farmers rather than follow a tribal way of life. The move succeeded in further undermining tribal traditions, but it did not improve living conditions for the Indians.

One Native American of the Progressive Era did much to improve government policies toward Indians. Henry Roe Cloud, the first Native American to graduate from Yale University, worked for what became the Brookings Institution, an organization dedicated to research in developing better social policies. There, he helped to bring attention to the terrible conditions on several Indian reservations. Roe Cloud was also active in the Bureau of Indian Affairs, a government agency. He created the American Indian Institute in 1915, the only school at the time that readied Native Americans for college instead of teaching them a trade.

Some Native American reforms seem less progressive today. Charles Curtis had grown up on an Indian reservation in Kansas. He was in favor of the Indian people adopting the ways of white society, which angered many tribal leaders. Curtis was a member of the House of Representatives from 1893 to 1907. He also wrote the Curtis Act, enacted in 1898, which did away with tribal governments and made many tribal land treaties worthless. However, Curtis later became the first Native American member of the Senate and led the Senate Committee on Indian Affairs in 1924. In that position, he spearheaded the Indian Citizenship Act, which allowed Indians to become U.S. citizens without losing their tribal rights.

The same was true in the mills, the mines, and the factories. Hours were long, with few or no breaks, and workplaces were crowded and dangerous.

The need for reform was clear. Wages needed to be increased, working conditions had to be improved, and people desperately needed to be helped out of the dirty, disease-ridden slums that had grown up in American cities.

Housing Reform in Cities

In the late 1800s and early 1900s, most poor people in cities lived in tenements, large buildings with many tiny apartments that had been hurriedly built by property owners of the 1800s in response to the growing population. New York's "railroad flats" were an example of this. The buildings, usually about six stories high, had four apartments squashed into an

There were no playgrounds apart from tenement yards and alleys in the city slums of the late 1800s and early 1900s. Housing conditions were particularly bad in New York City, seen here, where a huge population increase had strained the city to its limits. It was in New York that the first housing regulations were pushed into effect by social reformers.

area of 100 feet by 25 feet (30.5 m by 7.6 m) on each floor. Tiny rooms led like train compartments from one to the other with no hallways in between. There was little light, heat, or ventilation. The water was often undrinkable, and garbage and sewage filled the unpaved streets between the buildings. Tenement dwellers lived on poor diets and had no money for medicine. It was easy to get sick, and diseases spread quickly in the slums.

The progressive reformers of the late 1800s and early 1900s began a long struggle with local governments and city officials to introduce some control over housing conditions for poor people. The first federal report on housing conditions was published in 1894, but not until seven years later was a law passed enforcing housing regulations in one of the nation's cities. New York's "New Law" of 1901 created a housing department to carry out inspections and issue building permits. Property owners who did not comply with regulations could be fined. Slowly, regulations were introduced in other cities and states. Basic requirements were made regarding ventilation and plumbing, and cities invested in better sanitation and water systems.

The Labor Movement

By the late 1880s, it was commonplace for factories to be owned by large companies. The wealthy company owners did not always have the best interests of their workers at heart. Dismal working conditions motivated workers to join labor unions and fight for their rights. Naturally, the workers and the owners often had different ideas about what was best.

The labor unions were not always well organized and did not all agree on the same goals. Some unions were run by anarchists, or people who believe in freedom from government. Others were run by socialists, who believe that the government, and therefore the community it represents, should own businesses and industries rather than private individuals working for their own profit. Socialism had been introduced by recent European immigrants whose lives had been controlled for generations by rich property and business owners. The ideas of socialism worried many Americans, who believed this political system threatened liberty.

The strike, in which people refused to work until their demands for higher wages or better conditions were met, became the main weapon for unions. But the violence and rioting associated with strikes in the late 1800s had made many people nervous about union activity. Business leaders who opposed unions used their own tactics in response. They would ignore demands for increased wages—and even cut wages further—or they would simply fire workers who went on strike.

"[A union is] a miniature republic; its affairs were every man's affairs and every man had a real say about them."

Author Upton Sinclair

11

Even worse, employers responded with violence. In September 1913, a large group of about 9,000 coal miners went on strike for two reasons. First, they wanted to improve working conditions. Second, they wanted their employers to recognize the United Mine Workers' union, meaning that the company would listen to the union's demands and allow it to negotiate on behalf of union members. The workers and their families lived in homes owned by the Colorado Fuel and Iron Company. Expecting to be thrown out of their houses, they set up a village of tents in which to live. On April 20, 1914, the company sent armed guards to attack the workers' camp. The guardsmen first set fire to the tents and then shot down the workers and their families as they escaped. Between 18 and 20 were killed, including 13 children.

Eugene Debs (left) was a champion of the rights of working people and believed that socialism was the only way to achieve fairness and equality for everyone in society. This poster promotes Debs as the presidential candidate in 1904, on one of four occasions he ran for office.

The Unions Unite

One labor leader, Samuel Gompers, wanted to unite the labor movement and introduce some common policies. In 1886, he had founded the American Federation of Labor (AF of L), which brought together several craft unions, the unions that represented skilled and semi-skilled workers, or craftspeople. In the late 1890s, membership of the AF of L approached 400,000. Through Gompers' efforts, that number increased to more than 1.6 million by 1904. Gompers gained greater public acceptance for the union movement by focusing on real problems such as safety, hours of work, and rates of pay. He tried to steer workers away from conflict and extreme actions. But the violence surrounding union activity caused the AF of L to lose many members over the next several years.

Eugene V. Debs (1855–1926)

Eugene Victor Debs was born in Terre Haute, Indiana. A major force among labor leaders, he got his start when he was just 19 by organizing a local group of the Brotherhood of Locomotive Firemen.

In 1893, Debs organized the American Railway Union (ARU) and was its president until 1897. In 1894, under Debs's leadership, the ARU led a strike against the Pullman Palace Car Company to protest low wages. Thousands of ARU members showed their support by refusing to work on trains that used Pullman railway cars. The government ordered the strike to end, but the strikers refused. On July 7, 1894, National Guardsmen and police were called in. Hundreds of people were arrested, including Debs, and 13 died in the struggle. The Pullman strike was one of the most violent in America's history.

In 1897, Debs founded the Social Democratic party of America, which became part of the Socialist party in 1900. Debs's passionate but gentle manner made him a popular leader. He ran for president in 1900, 1904, 1908, and 1912 as the Socialist party candidate, but never won. In 1905, Debs helped found the Industrial Workers of the World, or Wobblies, dedicated to uniting both skilled and unskilled workers in one great union.

During World War I, Debs was arrested and sent to jail because he spoke out against the war. From his jail cell, he made a fifth attempt at becoming president. Although he received nearly a million votes, he was not successful. He was released from jail in 1921 and died five years later.

Another labor union movement emerged in 1905, led by William "Big Bill" Haywood and Socialist party leader Eugene Debs. Haywood and Debs founded the Industrial Workers of the World (IWW), also known as the Wobblies. They thought that there should be only one large union that included all workers, including unskilled laborers. The IWW opposed the AF of L because they felt it discriminated against the poorest workers by including only craftspeople. The Wobblies traveled the country, choosing cities in need of labor reform and making public speeches wherever they could find an audience.

"You can hope for no success on any policy of violence. . . . Violence . . . . means the loss of the strike."

Joe Ettor, IWW leader, speaking about a textile mill strike in Lawrence, Massachusetts, January 1912

Over the course of four years, Ida Tarbell tirelessly researched the actions of John D. Rockefeller and the power of his Standard Oil Company. First published as a series of articles in McClure's Magazine, and then in book form in 1904, Tarbell's History of the Standard Oil Company *exposed the company's dishonest practices. In 1911, the Supreme Court dissolved the company when it was shown that Standard Oil had unfairly driven its competition out of business.*

The Wobblies' greatest victory came in 1912, when they helped striking textile workers in Lawrence, Massachusetts, achieve their demands and brought national attention to the plight of the mill workers. The IWW received a lot of publicity, but its membership never equaled the high numbers reached by the AF of L.

Corruption Exposed

As the population and industrial world expanded, so did corruption among politicians, business people, and others who wanted to make money from the growing economy. Until the twentieth century, little was done to fight this corruption. In the early 1900s, however, a new breed of journalists appeared who used their profession to do just that. "Muckrakers" was the name given by President Theodore Roosevelt to this group of campaigners who uncovered wrongdoing and made it public.

The muckrakers exaggerated their stories somewhat to attract readers, but they were accomplished writers who truly cared about the welfare of their fellow Americans. They went into slaughterhouses, factories, and mills to investigate stories of danger and dishonesty. They scrutinized first the shady practices of business leaders and then went on to investigate politics and politicians.

One of the most famous muckrakers was a woman named Ida Tarbell. She and the other writers found an outlet for their investigations with Samuel Sydney McClure, owner of *McClure's Magazine.* Tarbell was one of his first writers; others included Willa Cather, Jack London, Rudyard Kipling, and Lincoln Steffens.

The Jungle

In 1906, author Upton Sinclair published *The Jungle*. In his book, this muckraker shed light on the terrible conditions inside the meatpacking industry in Chicago. Sinclair discovered a factory that was deliberately using not only decayed, diseased meat but pieces of food that had dropped to the floor. The factory included these in products such as sausages. The factory owners knowingly endangered people's health for the purpose of increasing profits.

What Sinclair described in *The Jungle* was likely to stop anyone from eating meat ever again, and his book became a best-seller. His campaigning work helped to promote both the Meat Inspection Act and the Pure Food and Drug Act of 1906. The Meat Inspection Act called for federal inspectors to approve the sanitary conditions in packing plants. The Pure Food and Drug Act was the first federal law that protected the American consumer by banning the manufacture and sale of spoiled or falsely labeled foods and drugs. Both acts were passed just six months after Sinclair's book was published.

Lincoln Steffens was a famous muckraker who concentrated on politics. He exposed a group of local politicians in St. Louis, Missouri, who were guilty of taking bribes from wealthy citizens in exchange for political favors. He went on to uncover and report on similar tales of corrupt politicians in several cities across the nation. *Cosmopolitan*, another magazine that supported the muckrakers' campaigns, published a series in 1906 entitled "The Treason of the Senate." These articles by David Graham Phillips featured corrupt senators. Phillips also published several books about the crumbling morals of society, including *The Great God Success* in 1901 and *The Conflict* in 1911.

"Capitalists, workingmen, politicians, citizens—all breaking the law, or letting it get broken."

McClure's Magazine, January 1903

Amidst a rash of questionable business and political practices, the muckrakers of the early 1900s did their part to right many wrongs. These writers brought widespread corruption to the attention of millions of Americans.

Investigative Journalism

The muckrakers were a new breed of reformers. Their words brought results, and their kind of investigative journalism has developed over the decades and still thrives today. Since 1900, journalists have exposed countless stories of corrupt practices.

One of the largest political scandals of the twentieth century was uncovered by the work of two journalists, Bob Woodward and Carl Bernstein of the Washington *Post*. They exposed serious wrongdoing by the Republican administration of President Richard Nixon with their report in 1972 of an illegal fund used to spy on and sabotage the Democratic party. The president was forced to resign because of the Watergate scandal, as it was known. Today, this kind of campaign is common, with scandals being reported by investigative journalists in newspapers and on television shows.

Many investigative campaigns have had very positive outcomes. For example, in 1979, a nuclear power plant on Three Mile Island in Pennsylvania released excess radiation when its reactor overheated. The company at first said it was a minor problem, but reporters refused to give up trying to find out what really happened. Eventually, the governor of Pennsylvania advised residents to evacuate. Because of all the attention concentrated on Three Mile Island, the federal government introduced significant new legislation to strengthen safety regulations in the nuclear power industry.

America's Stature Grows

A t the turn of the twentieth century, America was still extending and defining its borders. States were formed from existing territories and new territories were added. In the Spanish–American War of 1898, the United States had fought Spain over Spanish territories in the Caribbean and Pacific. The U.S. victory had helped to solidify the United States as a world power. America's economic power blossomed and three presidents furthered progress on both the domestic and international fronts.

Territories in North America

By 1853, the United States had acquired all of the North American continent south of Canada and north of Mexico. Between 1845 and 1890, most of its territories were admitted into the Union as states. Only three territories, all west of the Mississippi River, had yet to achieve statehood: New Mexico, Arizona, and Oklahoma.

The Indian Territory was the largest of the reservations set up by the U.S. government in the 1800s for Native Americans removed from their homelands. It had been divided in 1890 into Oklahoma Territory and a much-reduced Indian Territory. In 1907, the two were joined once more to become the state of Oklahoma. By the time Oklahoma became a state, Indians had lost much of their reservation land, and there were greater numbers of African Americans there than Indians. More all-black towns sprang up in Oklahoma than in all the rest of the nation at the time.

In 1912, the Western territories of Arizona and New Mexico became states. This meant that 48 states now formed the nation from coast to coast.

The United States also owned other territories. Farther north, the gold rush of the late 1890s had drawn attention to the potential of Alaska. Both the U.S., which owned Alaska, and Britain, which owned Canada, claimed areas along the boundary between southeastern Alaska and western Canada. Canadians believed a much earlier agreement between Britain and Russia gave them the right to important harbors in this region. But the harbors controlled the water routes to the Alaskan goldfields, and the United States believed it should have ownership of them. Theodore Roosevelt, who became president in 1901 upon the death of President William McKinley, felt the Alaska boundary dispute needed to be resolved. In 1903, government officials from both sides met in London, England, to solve the problem. The resulting compromise was in favor of the United States. Alaska was later organized as an American territory in 1912.

By 1912, after Arizona and New Mexico gained statehood, the 48 mainland United States were complete. In the Caribbean, America had acquired Puerto Rico as a territory in 1898. Cuba, although an independent nation from 1902, was still under the military protection of the United States. Another American protectorate was Panama, which had declared independence from Colombia in 1903.

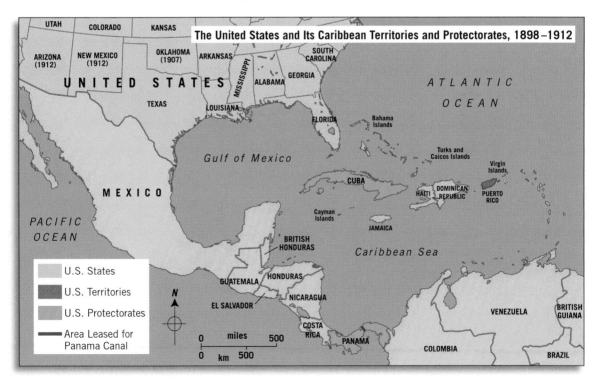

The United States and Its Caribbean Territories and Protectorates, 1898–1912

Expansion Abroad

Around the turn of the century, the United States acquired a significant amount of territory abroad. Puerto Rico (in the Caribbean) and the Philippine Islands and Guam (in the Pacific) were ceded to America in 1898 as a result of the Spanish–American War. Congress approved the annexation of Hawaii in 1898 and it became a U.S. territory in 1900. Several of the Samoan Islands, including Tutuila, became American Samoa in 1899, when a treaty between the U.S. and Germany divided the islands between the two nations.

The United States was interested in securing naval control of the Caribbean. To achieve this goal, President McKinley attempted to purchase the Virgin Islands (then called the

Alaska and Hawaii, which would later become the 49th and 50th states, were U.S. territories in 1912. So were several islands in the Pacific Ocean. The Philippines and Guam were ceded by Spain after the Spanish–American War in 1898. American Samoa (previously under the protection of Britain, Germany, and the United States) had become a U.S. territory in 1899.

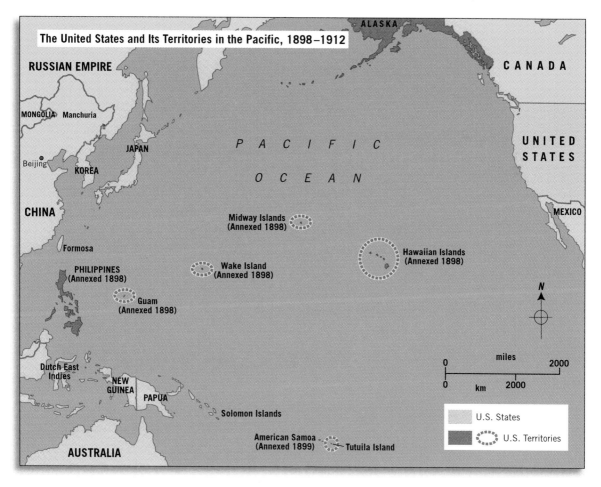

The United States and Its Territories in the Pacific, 1898–1912

ALASKA

RUSSIAN EMPIRE

CANADA

MONGOLIA Manchuria

JAPAN

Beijing KOREA

P A C I F I C

O C E A N

UNITED STATES

CHINA

MEXICO

Formosa

Midway Islands
(Annexed 1898)

Hawaiian Islands
(Annexed 1898)

PHILIPPINES
(Annexed 1898)

Wake Island
(Annexed 1898)

Guam
(Annexed 1898)

N

Dutch East
Indies

NEW
GUINEA

PAPUA

Solomon Islands

miles
0   2000
0   km   2000

American Samoa
(Annexed 1899)   Tutuila Island

AUSTRALIA

U.S. States

U.S. Territories

Danish West Indies) from Denmark at the turn of the century. The Senate approved the transaction but the Danish governing body did not. The Virgin Islands were eventually purchased by the United States from Denmark in 1917 for the price of $25 million.

The United States in Asia

During President McKinley's administration of 1897 to 1901, China lost a war with Japan and several major European nations quickly tried to seize Chinese territory for themselves. The U.S. Secretary of State, John Hay, was afraid that they would carve China into separately controlled pieces and, as a result, limit American trade there. In 1899, he declared an "Open Door" policy. The policy stated that all nations should be allowed to trade equally in China, and that no nation should interfere with another's trade there. Hay addressed a series of notes on the subject to U.S. ambassadors in Europe and Japan, instructing them to get approval from the other nations' leaders. None of the countries actually agreed in writing to his proposal, but the United States announced in 1900 that the Open Door policy was in effect.

The Chinese themselves, however, had other plans. On June 17, 1900, there was an uprising in China called the Boxer Rebellion, started by a secret revolutionary society called the Boxers. The main goal of the rebellion was to rid China of all foreigners. Forces were sent by the United States, Britain, France, Germany, Russia, and Japan to put a stop to the violence and relieve the Chinese capital of Beijing, which was under the control of the rebels.

A treaty, known as the Boxer Protocol, was signed in September 1901. This required China to pay more than $300 million over 40 years to other nations that had suffered losses due to the Boxer Rebellion. The United States only took $4 million of its $24.5 million share, and in 1908 committed the rest of the funds to scholarships for Chinese students in the U.S.

> "Within, the home market is secured; but outside, beyond the broad seas, there are the markets of the world, that can be entered or controlled only by a vigorous contest."
>
> *U.S. Navy Admiral Alfred Thayer Mahan*

The Square Deal

On September 6, 1901, President McKinley was attending a reception in Buffalo, New York, when he was killed by an assassin, Leon Czolgosz. Czolgosz said he killed the president in order to bring about change in the government. McKinley died on September 14 and was succeeded by Vice President Theodore Roosevelt.

At 42, "Teddy" Roosevelt was the youngest president ever to hold office. President Roosevelt was a strong leader and enthusiastic in his commitment to Progressive reform. His administration was relatively quiet until 1902, when he set out to reform the nation with what he called his "Square Deal." By this, he meant that all Americans should be given equal opportunities, whether they were rich or poor.

In 1902, Roosevelt decided to go after large businesses operating under powerful trusts. These trusts allowed companies to join forces, acquire a monopoly of certain industries, and get rid of all competition. Roosevelt's intention was to open the market to fair competition. He attacked J. P. Morgan's Northern Securities Company that owned three railroads. He also took action against Standard Oil and U.S. Steel, companies that dominated their industries.

Soon after, Roosevelt created the Department of Commerce and Labor. Within it was the Bureau of Corporations, the job of which was to "investigate companies [involved] in interstate commerce." Roosevelt had sent a message to the giants of business that government was not going to let them operate as they pleased if it was not healthy for the nation. This was a victory for the Progressives, who had long campaigned for stronger laws to protect poorer Americans against the abuses of big businesses.

> "We must treat each man on his worth and merits as a man. We must see that each is given a square deal, because he is entitled to no more and should receive no less."
>
> *President Theodore Roosevelt, 1902*

Roosevelt Pioneers Conservation

In 1900, America was already losing some of its most precious natural resources due to rapid westward expansion. Natural habitats for wildlife were disappearing and certain

21

species were becoming endangered. Roosevelt had a deep love for the natural beauty of his country and was a true pioneer of conservation. As president, he established the country's first wildlife refuges.

The Antiquities Act of 1906 allowed the government to protect regions deemed to be of special interest or importance. Under this act, many national parks and

John Muir (1838–1914)

In his passionate efforts to save natural habitats for wildlife and plant species, John Muir became one of America's most important environmentalists. His life was dedicated to educating people about the environment and conserving America's resources.

Born in Scotland, Muir moved to Wisconsin as a young boy. He was very bright and was always inventing interesting things. When he was 29, an accident left him temporarily blind. After regaining his sight, he also gained an appreciation of the natural world. He ventured into the wilderness, learning as much as he could about the Earth and calling himself a "citizen of the Earth-planet-universe."

In 1892, Muir cofounded the Sierra Club to protect wildlife and the environment. It is still in existence today. With his deep love of nature and

understanding of science, Muir wrote about the importance of preserving the natural world. In 1901, his book *Our National Parks* caught the eye of President Roosevelt. In 1903, Muir and Roosevelt spent four days together in Yosemite, California. From this meeting, Roosevelt was convinced that dramatic action needed to be taken to protect America's natural beauty. Muir lived to see the creation of many nationally protected sites that resulted in part from his time with Roosevelt.

monuments were established. Devil's Tower, an unusual landform in Wyoming, became the nation's first national monument in 1906. In all, Roosevelt designated 18 nationally protected areas.

The forests were a natural resource desperately in need of help, as lumber companies stripped the landscape of trees to meet the growing demand for building materials, fuel, and paper products. At the beginning of Roosevelt's presidency, there were 47 million acres of national forests. Because of his perseverance, America had 195 million acres of national forests by the time Roosevelt left office.

Roosevelt was responsible for the National Reclamation Act in 1902, which started federal irrigation projects to replenish dry areas. It also allowed for the building of some of the greatest dams in the West.

Yosemite Valley in California, one of America's most beautiful areas, was preserved for the nation in 1906, when it became a national park. It remains both a natural habitat for wildlife and a popular destination for visitors.

"Big Stick" Diplomacy

Roosevelt believed the United States should maintain a position of power in the world. He was not one to think that America should stay isolated within its shores and he understood that progress in communications and transportation would continue to make the world a smaller place. Roosevelt wanted the nation to be a leader in foreign affairs, and he practiced what became known as "big stick" diplomacy. This meant the threat of American power was present in negotiations with other countries, even though it remained unspoken.

In 1902, Roosevelt used the "big stick" when he intervened in the Caribbean. At the time, Britain, Germany, and Italy were in conflict with Venezuela, on the Caribbean coast of South America, over loans that Venezuela had not repaid.

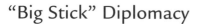

"There is nothing in the world more beautiful than Yosemite . . . and the people should see to it that [it is] preserved for their children and their children's children."

President Theodore Roosevelt

Theodore Roosevelt (1858–1919)

Theodore Roosevelt was born in New York City to a prominent family. He went to Harvard University in 1876 and married Alice Hathaway Lee in 1880. Roosevelt's first job in politics was in the New York state legislature. But in 1884, after the deaths of both his wife and his mother, he decided not to run for reelection.

In December 1886, Roosevelt married Edith Carow. Three years later, he stepped back into the world of politics with a job on the Civil Service Commission under President Benjamin Harrison. This job was followed with the position of New York City police commissioner.

President Roosevelt takes office in 1905.

In 1897, President McKinley made him assistant secretary of the United States Navy. When the Spanish–American War began in 1898, Roosevelt helped gather together a regiment of volunteers known as the "Rough Riders," and went off to fight the war. His heroic contribution to that fight put him in the spotlight. In 1898, he became governor of New York State.

Roosevelt was nominated for vice president in 1900. When President McKinley was killed in 1901, Roosevelt succeeded him as president. He was a dynamic president who brought about reform of big business and raised awareness of environmental issues. Roosevelt also expressed publicly his distaste for racial inequality in American society. And in 1906, Roosevelt was awarded the Nobel Peace Prize because of talks he had organized between the warring nations of Russia and Japan.

Regretting his decision not to run for a third term as president, Roosevelt started the Bull Moose party and entered the election of 1912. He gained over 4 million votes, but was defeated by Woodrow Wilson.

This cartoon is entitled "The Big Stick in the Caribbean Sea." It shows Roosevelt leading his mighty navy in 1904, by which time his "big stick" diplomacy had affected the nations and islands of the Caribbean.

The European nations began bombing and blockading Venezuelan ports. Roosevelt was concerned that Europeans were on the verge of violating the Monroe Doctrine. This U.S. declaration, made in 1823, warned European nations against colonizing or interfering in the Americas. Roosevelt successfully negotiated a peaceful settlement.

Roosevelt believed that the United States had a duty to help other nations in times of crisis. Even more, he intended to protect American economic interests in other countries. During his presidency, Roosevelt took steps to strengthen the United States Army and Navy. In December 1907, the navy embarked on a "goodwill cruise," actually a show of strength to the rest of the world and especially to Japan. The "Great White Fleet" sailed around the world until early 1909.

"I have always been fond of the West African proverb, 'Speak softly and carry a big stick; you will go far.'"

Theodore Roosevelt, 1900

Panama

The Panama Canal was a controversial project that may never have come into being without Roosevelt's strong will and support. The aim of the canal was to connect the Atlantic and Pacific Oceans by carving a deep water channel through Panama, then a province of Colombia. (See map on page 18.) This would create a valuable transportation route to be maintained and controlled by the United States. Colombia would give up control over the canal zone and, in return, the U.S. would pay Colombia $10 million up front and an annual rent of $250,000. However, in 1903, the Colombian government refused to approve the project, hoping to receive more money by holding out.

Roosevelt reacted strongly, and considered seizing Panama by force. Instead, on November 3, 1903, the province of Panama, with the help of foreign forces and the approval of the United States, revolted against Colombia and declared its independence. U.S. Navy warships were already in the region and served to protect the Panamanians from any military action by Colombia. On November 6, the United States recognized the new Republic of Panama. The Hay-Bunau-Varilla Treaty with Panama, agreed a few days later, gave the United States full control over a canal zone ten miles (16 km) wide. It was passed by Congress in 1904.

The events in Panama angered many South American nations, as they did not believe the United States should become involved in affairs south of its border. It also caused dispute at home, since U.S. involvement in Panama was clearly for financial reasons rather than to help Panamanians. Nevertheless, the Panama Canal project went forward.

President Taft

Theodore Roosevelt was an influential, successful president, admired and loved by many. However, he declined to run for a third term. On March 4, 1909, Republican William Howard Taft became America's 27th president, having defeated the Democratic candidate William Jennings Bryan.

Taft was even more determined than Roosevelt to defeat the powerful trusts, or monopolies. In one term as president, Taft took legal action against the monopolies twice as many times as Roosevelt had in two terms. But after the dynamic presidency of Roosevelt, Taft's accomplishments went

William Howard Taft (1857–1930)

William Howard Taft was born in Washington, D.C. He attended Yale University and then Cincinnati Law College in Ohio, graduating in 1880.

In 1881, Taft became a prosecuting attorney for the city of Cincinnati, and then served as a judge on the Cincinnati Supreme Court. He became an attorney for the federal government in 1890. In 1900, President William McKinley put Taft in charge of creating a government in the Philippine Islands. Taft became the Philippines' first American governor.

In 1903, President Roosevelt named Taft as secretary of war. When Roosevelt chose not to run in 1908, he supported Taft to succeed him as president. During his presidency, Taft continued Roosevelt's campaign against the monopolies and cut back on government spending. He also introduced the idea of a national budget, or spending plan, which was eventually adopted in 1921. After his term as president, Taft took a position at Yale teaching law. In 1920, President Warren Harding offered Taft a position on the U.S. Supreme Court, a job he had long wanted. He served for ten years before his death in 1930. Taft was the only person ever to serve as both president and a Supreme Court justice.

somewhat unnoticed by Americans. He lost the 1912 presidential election to the Democrat Woodrow Wilson.

President Wilson Aims High

Woodrow Wilson had many ideas that he was eager to pursue. He instantly began a plan for reform that he called the "New Freedom." Part of this plan was the Federal Reserve Act, passed in 1913, which created a centralized banking system for the nation. The Federal Reserve, still in place today, regulates the flow of money in the United States in an effort to keep the economy stable.

Also in 1913, Congress approved the Underwood Tariff Act. It was a major victory for Wilson, lowering taxes he had

> "America is not now, and cannot in the future be, a place for unrestricted individual enterprise."
>
> *Woodrow Wilson, on the need to reform big business, 1912*

long felt needed to be reduced. In 1914, a congressional study showed that "the final control of American industry rests . . . in the hands of a small number of wealthy and powerful financiers." Because of this, a Federal Trade Commission was established and the Clayton Antitrust Act was passed. Both actions were taken to prevent monopolies and other unfair business practices.

President Wilson was concerned with protecting the rights of American citizens. He fought to ban products made by child laborers and helped the economic situation of farmers. Wilson also secured an eight-hour workday for railroad workers, who previously had to work whatever long hours their employers demanded. The Adamson Act of 1916 that achieved this change was implemented to stop disputes on the railroads, but it paved the way for a standard eight-hour day for all workers.

The Teddy Bear is Born

Although Teddy Roosevelt was an avid hunter, on one particular hunting trip in 1902 he refused to shoot a small, helpless bear. News of this event was published in the form of a cartoon in the Washington *Post*.

The cartoon inspired store owner Morris Mitchom in Brooklyn, New York, to create a toy bear. He placed it in his window with a sign that said "Teddy's Bear." As the story goes, the bears sold out quickly, creating a demand for more. Mitchom sent a bear to the president requesting his permission to call them "teddy bears."

The teddy bear was born and Mitchom became extremely wealthy. The toy became a classic American and international favorite, and is still produced by the millions. The first teddy bear that was made in Brooklyn is housed in the National Museum of American History in Washington, D.C.

One of the earliest teddy bears, made in about 1904.

War Breaks Out

While the United States was moving forward in the Progressive Era, the atmosphere in Europe was turbulent. Nationalism—a fierce loyalty to one's country and culture—was on the rise. And at the turn of the century, there was a delicate balance of power in Europe. Military alliances divided the continent into two main camps.

European Balance of Power

In a military alliance, when one country has a conflict with another, the allied nations agree either to lend assistance or remain neutral. At the time, people thought military alliances offered protection against war. These alliances, in reality, offered a false sense of security. They also complicated political matters in Europe.

In 1871, after France fought Germany in the Franco–Prussian War, a unified Germany became the leading power on the European continent. The former French provinces of Alsace and Lorraine were in German hands and an angry France waited for the opportunity to reclaim its prewar power.

Germany, on the other hand, set out to establish alliances to secure its political and military might. The nation's prime minister, Otto von Bismarck, created an alliance with Austria-Hungary in 1879. The two countries agreed to go to war if Russia attacked either one. In 1882, Italy joined forces with Germany and Austria-Hungary. Like Germany, Italy had recently achieved unification and was seeking to expand its territory. These three nations were linked in what was known as the Triple Alliance.

In 1894, France and Russia agreed to ready their troops if any nation in the Triple Alliance did the same. They also agreed to help each other should Germany attack either nation. This pact was called the Double Entente. (*Entente* is French for "agreement.")

Meanwhile, German forces grew dramatically and Germany's navy increased to rival that of the British. This caused tension across the English Channel, where Britain no longer felt safe standing alone, and led in 1904 to an agreement between Britain and France called the Entente Cordiale. In 1907, Russia joined the Entente Cordiale and the group became the Triple Entente. This complex system of alliances would entangle all of Europe in World War I.

Nationalism and Militarism

The wave of nationalism that was spreading throughout Europe strengthened the unity within several nations, such as Germany and Italy. The people in these countries had a common language, culture, history, and religion. They believed in their own nations' goals, and their nationalism would inspire citizens to fight other countries.

However, some Eastern Europeans were not as united by national spirit. Large nations and empires such as Russia, the Ottoman Empire (ruled by the Turks), and Austria-Hungary were made up of smaller cultural groups that were hostile to each other and wanted to remain independent. For example, the Slavic people living in the Austro-Hungarian provinces of Bosnia and Herzegovina resented being ruled by Austria-Hungary. They wanted to be part of Serbia, a nation that became independent in the 1800s after centuries of control by the Ottoman Turks. Serbia itself wanted to control these Slavic areas, and therefore posed a threat to Austria-Hungary.

Circumstances were complicated further by the fact that the Ottoman Empire was extremely unstable. Not only Serbia, but the other Balkan states of Rumania, Bulgaria, and Greece had broken away from the empire to become separate nations. A war in this region had eliminated Turkish control

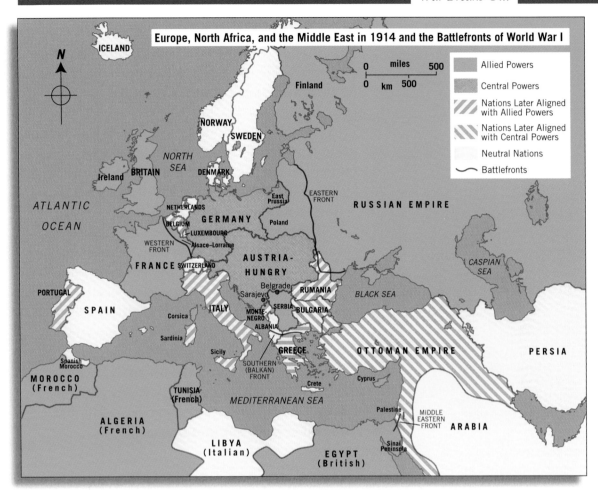

Europe, North Africa, and the Middle East in 1914 and the Battlefronts of World War I

N

ICELAND

miles 500

km 500

Allied Powers

Central Powers

Nations Later Aligned with Allied Powers

Nations Later Aligned with Central Powers

Neutral Nations

Battlefronts

Finland

NORWAY

SWEDEN

NORTH SEA

DENMARK

East Prussia

EASTERN FRONT

RUSSIAN EMPIRE

Ireland BRITAIN

ATLANTIC OCEAN

NETHERLANDS

BELGIUM GERMANY Poland

LUXEMBOURG

WESTERN FRONT Alsace–Lorraine

FRANCE SWITZERLAND

AUSTRIA-HUNGRY

CASPIAN SEA

PORTUGAL

SPAIN

Corsica

ITALY

Belgrade
Sarajevo

MONTE-NEGRO SERBIA

ALBANIA

RUMANIA

BULGARIA

BLACK SEA

Sardinia

Sicily

GREECE

SOUTHERN (BALKAN) FRONT

Crete

OTTOMAN EMPIRE

Cyprus

PERSIA

Spanish Morocco

MOROCCO (French)

TUNISIA (French)

MEDITERRANEAN SEA

Palestine

MIDDLE EASTERN FRONT ARABIA

ALGERIA (French)

LIBYA (Italian)

EGYPT (British)

Sinai Peninsula

and left the region vulnerable to two nations that had long wanted to claim it: Russia and Austria-Hungary. In addition, a Japanese victory over Russia in 1905 motivated the Russians to rebuild their powerful image. It also caused Russia to turn away from the Far East and focus instead on expansion within Europe, especially the Balkans.

Nationalism also inspired militarism, which is a nation's efforts to increase its military might. People wanted their countries to be strong and self-sufficient. France, Russia, Austria-Hungary, and Germany all concentrated on building up their armies. By 1913, Germany had the strongest, largest army in the world. Europe was a powder keg poised for conflict, and one action was about to ignite the short fuse.

This map shows the countries of Europe in 1914, and how the most powerful nations became two opposing groups, the Central Powers and the Allied Powers, at the beginning of World War 1. It also shows other nations that joined in the conflict and those that stayed neutral as the battlefronts spread across Europe into the Middle East and Africa.

Assassination of an Archduke

Archduke Franz Ferdinand was heir to the throne of Austria-Hungary. To the Slavic people of Bosnia, he was a symbol of unjust dominance over their region. In 1914, the archduke traveled to Sarajevo, the capital city of Bosnia, to look over the Austrian troops stationed there. As he and his wife Sophie rode through the city on June 28, an assassin, 19-year-old Gavrilo Princip, fired two shots. Both the archduke and his wife were killed.

The murder of the archduke and his wife gave Austria-Hungary the reason they were looking for to put pressure on Serbia. Determined to crush the small nation, Austria-Hungary first secured support from Germany. Then, on July 23, 1914, a list of impossible demands was sent to the Serbians. They were given only 48 hours to respond. Although Serbia agreed to most of the demands, Austria-Hungary was not satisfied. In fact, the list was designed to be unacceptable, since Austria-Hungary wanted to go to war with Serbia.

Archduke Franz Ferdinand of Austria-Hungary and his wife Sophie, whose deaths set World War I in motion. The archduke's assassin, Gavrilo Princip, along with the nationalist Serb group to which he belonged, was not aware that Ferdinand was sympathetic to the desires of the Slavic people and had planned to give them their independence once he became ruler.

War Is Declared

Austria-Hungary declared war on Serbia on July 28, 1914. Russia sprang to Serbia's defense and mobilized troops along the border of Serbia. Germany, led by the power-hungry Kaiser Wilhelm II, responded by declaring war on Russia on August 1. On August 3, Germany declared war on France, as that nation was an ally of Russia. Italy, the third member of the Triple Alliance, did not join forces with Germany and Austria-Hungary.

The following day, on August 4, German forces invaded France by going through Belgium. This angered Belgium, which was a neutral nation. Britain was the official protector of Belgium's neutrality, and so Germany's invasion of Belgium drew the British into the war. Britain declared war on Germany that same day.

World War I had been set in motion. The nations of the Triple Entente and their empires became known as the Allies. The Triple Alliance countries were now called the Central Powers. The system of alliances, originally intended to secure peace, had brought nearly all of Europe into the conflict.

As the years passed, the war in Europe continued. There were three major European fronts on which the battle was fought: the western, the eastern, and the southern. (See map on page 31.) The western front extended from the western border of Switzerland to the North Sea. The eastern front involved Russia. The southern, or Balkan, front was in Serbia. The war was also fought in the Middle East and Africa, with the British advancing from Egypt into the Ottoman Empire.

Japan had quickly entered the war on the Allied side, with the hope of gaining territory in German-occupied parts of China and the Pacific. Italy joined the Allies in May 1915, and Bulgaria joined the Central Powers in September. The Serbian capital of Belgrade fell to the Central Powers the following month. That same year, there was fighting in the German colonies in Africa, New Guinea, and Samoa. The war had truly become global.

America Tries to Stay Neutral

When war broke out in Europe, there were approximately 120,000 Americans there. Most of them immediately returned to the United States. In general, the feeling in America was against becoming embroiled in a European conflict. President Wilson initially called the war "a distant event" and asked Americans to stay "impartial [not taking sides] in thought as well as in action."

For two and a half years, the United States officially remained neutral. Less than a year into the war, however, American opinion started to change. On May 7, 1915, a German submarine sank the British steamship *Lusitania*. The *Lusitania* was traveling from New York City to Liverpool, England. Of the nearly 1,200 people killed, 128 were Americans. The situation, however, was not as

> "The lamps are going out all over Europe; we shall not see them lit again in our lifetime."
>
> *British Foreign Minister Sir Edward Grey at the start of World War I*

straightforward as it may seem, because the German embassy had forewarned passengers of danger. Those aboard the steamship knew they would be entering hostile waters and were traveling at their own risk.

Americans were divided on the issue of entering the war. Many Americans were angered after the *Lusitania* incident and began to favor entering the war on the side of the Allies. Nevertheless, Wilson remained firm in his declaration of neutrality. Others also wanted to remain neutral, but there were mixed loyalties among immigrants in the United States. There were millions of Americans of German descent, but there were also large numbers of British immigrants and their descendants. In addition, there were American businessmen

Woodrow Wilson (1856–1924)

Thomas Woodrow Wilson was born in Virginia. He graduated from Princeton University in 1879 and became a lawyer in 1882, after attending law school at the University of Virginia. Wilson soon discovered that he did not like being a lawyer and went back to school to study political science. He got his degree from Johns Hopkins University in 1886.

Wilson had a successful career as a professor and, later, as president of Princeton University. After leaving Princeton in 1910, Wilson was elected governor of New Jersey. His strong leadership resulted in his being chosen as Democratic candidate for president in the 1912 election. Wilson easily beat the Republican candidate, President Taft.

As president, Wilson implemented important economic and social reforms. He was most concerned with achieving the ideals of democracy that the nation's founders had set forth and helping other nations do the same. During World War I, Wilson's famous "Fourteen Points" speech suggested the creation of a League of Nations and paved the way for peace. He went on to play an important part in the peace talks that resulted in the Treaty of Versailles. Wilson was disappointed when Congress refused to join the League of Nations or sign the treaty, but his contribution had a profound and lasting impact on the world. In 1919, he received the Nobel Peace Prize for his work.

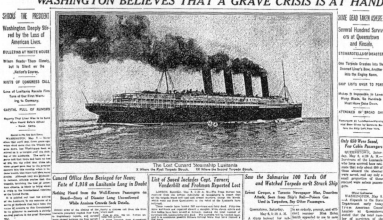

"All the News That's Fit to Print."

The New York Times.

EXTRA 5:30 A.M.

VOL. LXIV...NO. 20,888.   NEW YORK, SATURDAY, MAY 8, 1915.—TWENTY-FOUR PAGES.   ONE CENT

LUSITANIA SUNK BY A SUBMARINE, PROBABLY 1,260 DEAD; TWICE TORPEDOED OFF IRISH COAST; SINKS IN 15 MINUTES; CAPT. TURNER SAVED, FROHMAN AND VANDERBILT MISSING; WASHINGTON BELIEVES THAT A GRAVE CRISIS IS AT HAND

The Lost Cunard Steamship Lusitania

On May 8, 1915, the front page of The New York Times *reported the sinking of the Lusitania. More than half of the 1,918 people on board had died. President Wilson issued a statement saying that the prior warning given by the Germans was no excuse for the loss of life in this "unlawful and inhumane act."*

who saw the war as an opportunity for profit, especially if they could trade with all the participants.

Under the campaign slogan "He kept us out of war," Wilson won reelection in the 1916 presidential race. Wilson's opponents criticized him for being cowardly and avoiding confrontation. But Wilson was not so much afraid of war as he was dedicated to fostering peace. He believed strongly in diplomacy and democracy.

Wilson tried to arrange peace talks between the warring nations in 1915. The president also protested repeatedly to Germany about submarine attacks on passenger liners. In spring 1916, he issued a threat: U.S. relations with Germany would be severed unless this was stopped. For a time, the Germans did stop sinking passenger ships without warning.

In December 1916, Wilson asked the countries at war to state their terms for peace, but there was no response. Also in 1916, Wilson ordered Admiral William S. Sims of the United States Navy to take command of the American naval forces in Europe.

"To all U-boats— sink on sight."

Order sent to German submarines, February 1, 1917

William S. Sims (1858–1936)

William S. Sims was born in Canada. His family moved to the United States when he was 13, eventually settling in Pennsylvania. Sims graduated from the U.S. Naval Academy in 1880 and set out on a naval career that would span 42 years. Sims became a gunnery expert and a stickler for safety. Throughout his career, he dedicated himself to serious reforms in the United States Navy.

Sims moved up the ranks over the years and was made rear admiral in 1916. Just a few months later, President Wilson sent him to London to arrange for cooperation between the American and British navies. He was put in command of the American naval forces in Europe. Before Sims reached England, the United States had declared war on Germany.

Sims reasoned that to stop the destructive German submarine warfare from wiping out the British fleet, a convoy system was needed. Instead of having a single ship set off across the ocean, many ships should travel together, encircled by destroyers, or small warships. This strategy was immediately successful, saving the British naval forces from certain destruction. Many historians

Admiral Sims arriving in North Africa during World War I.

believe that World War I would have been lost without Sims.

After the war, Sims became the president of the Naval War College in Providence, Rhode Island. In 1921, he won the Pulitzer Prize for history with his book *The Victory at Sea*.

The United States Enters the War

On February 1, 1917, the Germans renewed their use of submarine warfare. Although German leaders knew this probably meant engaging the United States in war, they were hoping for a quick victory before the Americans could effectively mobilize their forces. Wilson immediately broke off relations with Germany.

Another incident increased tension between America and Germany in early 1917. Arthur Zimmerman, Germany's foreign minister, sent a message to the German ambassador in Mexico on January 16. The message was intercepted and decoded by British intelligence. In essence, the Zimmerman telegram offered Mexico an alliance with Germany if it would start a war with America. When this information was relayed to the American people on March 1, it helped to sway opinion in favor of entering the war.

On March 16, 1917, the Germans torpedoed two American ships. With that, U.S. neutrality was over. On April 2, President Wilson asked Congress for a declaration of war. Congress responded on April 6, and America was at war with the Central Powers.

President Woodrow Wilson addresses a packed Congress on April 2, 1917, to request a declaration of war against Germany. At this point, Wilson had done all he could to protest the war in Europe and find a peaceful remedy to the three-year-old conflict.

"The world must be made safe for democracy."

President Wilson's address to Congress, April 2, 1917

A New Kind of War

World War I was unique for many reasons. It was the first major war to be fought with new technology that made it possible to carry on conflicts for longer periods of time and with greater casualties. The Industrial Age of the 1800s had produced barbed wire, rapid-fire machine guns, and more efficient ways to communicate, travel, and preserve food.

Daily life for soldiers was particularly gruesome and miserable in the trenches. These were ditches cut into the ground from which troops would attack the enemy and defend themselves. Soldiers might spend months at a time living and fighting in trenches.

A British fighter (foreground) battles with German planes in the sky over the western front. The airplane was first introduced as a weapon of war in World War I.

Weapons such as poison gas were new instruments of misery; and tanks, used to barrel through the dugout trenches and barbed wire, were also a product of World War I. Another factor made World War I deadlier than any war before it. In most earlier European conflicts, nations had primarily fought each other one on one. World War I was the first conflict in which many nations fought on multiple fronts that spanned a large area of the world. The fighting spread from Western Europe all the way to the Middle East and Africa. Over the course of four years, nearly 10 million soldiers lost their lives.

The global way in which World War I was fought affected warfare forever. Multinational alliances have become extremely complex and include many goals and viewpoints. In addition, as technology continues to advance, the risks become increasingly dangerous. Weapons become ever more powerful and far reaching. A world war fought today would almost certainly involve nuclear power and deadly chemical weapons.

4

The American Contribution

W hen the time came to go to war, U.S. forces were not at their peak. There were only about 128,000 men in the army and there was no one yet in charge of leading the troops overseas. A scramble took place to assemble enough soldiers and to raise sufficient funds for the war effort.

Economic Efforts

The United States needed billions of dollars to equip its armed forces and transport them overseas, send supplies to the Allies, and build factories to make war materials. Several programs were created to raise the necessary money.

Wilson put Bernard Baruch in charge of the War Industries Board in March 1918. Baruch's job was to direct industries to produce war materials. He was a businessman and knew how to deal with other businessmen. Since the War Industries Board was also responsible for doling out scarce resources, such as coal and steel, Baruch used this to persuade them to cooperate.

In 1917, women entered the workforce in new roles, both to replace men who went to war and to assist in the manufacture of military supplies. These women are welding bomb casings in a munitions factory. Existing factories were converted and new ones built in the United States to produce weapons for the war in Europe.

Baruch successfully persuaded industrial leaders to conserve vital resources, limit steel prices, cut back on production of pleasure cars, and take other measures that increased the overall efficiency of industry. The astonishing level of production that resulted included 3 million rifles, 22 million blankets, more than 5 million gas masks, and nearly 35 million pairs of boots and shoes. Trucks, trains, and communications equipment were also produced.

There were some problems. Production was slow while new factories were constructed, and there was little time for industries to shift from fulfilling the needs of consumers to supplying the military. As a result, there was a shortage of U.S. planes and ships throughout the war.

> "Our minds have met and I have the utmost confidence in your judgement."
>
> *President Wilson to Bernard Baruch during World War I*

The U.S. Food Administration, led by Herbert Hoover, produced posters as part of a campaign to conserve food for the war effort. This woman in Mobile, Alabama, is attaching a poster to a cart, hoping to encourage American women to think of those in Europe.

Americans Support the Effort

To raise war funds, taxes were increased and applied to a wider range of people. Income tax and other taxes, such as those imposed on business, raised nearly $3.7 billion for the government in 1918. Another staggering $23 billion poured in from the sale of war bonds and war savings certificates.

People also supported the war effort by taking part in "meatless and wheatless" days in order to make more food available to send to troops and civilians in Europe. Herbert Hoover headed this campaign to save food, but the voluntary efforts of American citizens were not enough. As U.S. Food Administrator, Hoover was given the power to control what portion of farm production should go directly to American and Allied forces. In addition, Hoover needed to regulate prices so that inflation did not become a problem.

Liberty Bonds

Soon after the United States entered the war, the government began to sell war bonds to help raise funds. People purchased war bonds—known also as Liberty or Victory bonds—as a way of loaning the government money. The bonds were certificates promising repayment to people who lent money by buying them. When the time came to cash in the bonds after the war, that money would be repaid with interest, or extra money on top of the original amount of the loan.

Hundreds of celebrities used their fame to sell Liberty bonds. In one spectacular gathering in New York City, movie stars Charlie Chaplin, Mary Pickford, and Douglas Fairbanks all appealed to Americans to buy bonds. Chaplin told the crowd of 30,000, "Remember, each bond you buy will save a soldier's life—and a mother's son!—will bring this war to an early victory!"

Many rallies were held, volunteers paraded through city neighborhoods, and President Wilson even promoted the bonds at a Broadway show. Young children joined in by buying Liberty stamps to save in stamp booklets. Once a child had filled up a booklet, he or she would receive a Liberty bond.

Movie star Mary Pickford encourages a crowd to buy Liberty bonds at a rally in New York City during World War I.

"Americans are the most cooperative people in the world."

Herbert Hoover, on the U.S. war effort

This recruiting poster persuaded millions of Americans to volunteer for military service in World War I. It became a famous image and was used again every time the United States became involved in a war.

Government regulations for the use of transportation and fuel were introduced. Secretary of the Treasury William G. McAdoo was put in charge of the nation's railroads. And Harry Garfield, named Fuel Administrator, created a program to conserve energy. Voluntary efforts were considerable, as people observed "gasless Sundays," and coal was conserved on "heatless Mondays." Children collected peach pits that were used to make charcoal filters for gas masks. Women and children knitted sweaters and socks for the Red Cross to send to soldiers.

Preparing to Fight

Immediate measures were necessary to add as many soldiers as possible to the U.S. forces. America had usually relied on volunteers for the armed forces, but a draft was now needed. Congress passed the Selective Service Act on May 17, 1917, requiring all men between the ages of 21 and 30 to register for military duty. By the time World War I was over, the draft had been extended to include those between 18 and 45. Men of all ages also volunteered, as did many women. Women enlisted primarily as nurses and administrators. Of the 24 million people who registered for service during the war, about 5 million were volunteers. A lottery decided who among those registered would actually serve.

There was little resistance to the draft, and neighbors reported those who did try to "dodge" registering. The dark side of this fierce patriotism was a kind of war

I WANT YOU
FOR U.S. ARMY
NEAREST RECRUITING STATION

hysteria. Many men who were suspected of draft dodging were rounded up and brought to police stations all over the country. Tragically, some incidents turned violent. In addition, propaganda and anti-German feeling ran like wildfire through America. German Americans, regardless of their loyalties, were treated harshly and the German language was no longer taught in some schools.

The government reacted severely to anyone it decided was acting against United States interests. The Espionage Act of 1917 and the Sedition Act of 1918 both brought severe penalties to anyone who was "disloyal, profane, scurrilous, or abusive" regarding the United States. The laws were used many times to punish people who spoke out against the war.

The AEF and the Supreme War Council

Although the U.S. had joined the war to help the Allies, it was not officially on the Allied team. American forces went to Europe as the American Expeditionary Force (AEF). General John "Black Jack" Pershing was appointed as its commander in chief.

The AEF had a slow start. After arriving in France in June 1917 with the first troops, Pershing began training his inexperienced soldiers. By November, a few hundred thousand were ready to fight, but the Americans would not see much combat until 1918.

Millions registered for service during World War I, but they had no experience of combat and were unprepared for the harsh realities that would face them on the battlefield. This soldier, a member of the New York National Guard, was leaving for training in South Carolina before being sent overseas.

"It is horrible beyond the power of words to express, to think that the civilized world should suffer such bloodshed and destruction."

General John Pershing, speaking about World War I

In 1917, Italy was beginning to crumble at the hands of the Austrians and Germans. And in Russia, a revolutionary named Vladimir Lenin took power. Lenin was a communist, meaning he followed a political system in which all resources and property are owned by the nation, or people, as a whole rather than privately by individuals. Lenin established communist rule in Russia and signed an armistice with the Central Powers on December 15, 1917.

Without Italy and Russia, the Allies felt they needed to coordinate their remaining resources to act more effectively. In November 1917, at a meeting in Rapallo, Italy, the Supreme War Council was established. It would act as a unified military command for the Allies because the separate commands were not functioning smoothly enough to ensure victory. The

John Joseph Pershing (1860–1948)

John Joseph Pershing was born in Laclede, Missouri. He graduated from West Point Military Academy in 1882. Pershing got his nickname "Black Jack" from commanding African American soldiers in Cuba during the Spanish-American War in 1898. In 1916, he was promoted to major general. The following year, America entered World War I and Pershing was appointed commander of the American Expeditionary Force in Europe.

Pershing was known as a solemn, tough, and stern leader. In keeping with his orders, he fought to keep American soldiers solely under his command, and only agreed to send them into British or French sectors when it was absolutely necessary.

After the war, Pershing was promoted twice, becoming chief of staff in 1921. He retired from the army three years later. Pershing published his memoirs, entitled *My Experiences in the World War*, in 1931.

pressure was on for America to join the unified forces, but Pershing held firm. He would send troops where they were needed, but was determined to keep the AEF independent.

Admiral William S. Sims was already leading American naval forces in Europe. The United States Navy took action within a month of going to war and worked in cooperation with the British Royal Navy. Under Sims's leadership, U.S. naval forces used convoys and American destroyers to help counter German submarine warfare.

Wilson's Fourteen Points

By January 1918, it became clear to all the major powers that the time would soon come for negotiating peace. On January 5, British Prime Minister David Lloyd George announced the terms on which his nation would agree to end the war. The Germans rejected them outright.

The world knew that President Wilson had brought the United States into World War I with reluctance. He was by nature a man of peace, and his main priority was negotiating to that end. In his message to Congress on January 8, 1918, Wilson outlined his vision in his "Fourteen Points" speech.

The first four points focused on general issues such as freedom of the seas, reduction of weapons, equal trade, and no secret international agreements. The fifth point said that the citizens of colonies should have a say in who governed them equal to that of the nations that claimed control over them. The next eight were specific territorial and political issues, such as the evacuation of German troops from several occupied nations and limited self-government for the varied peoples of Austria-Hungary.

In his last point, Wilson talked about a community of nations that would maintain peace throughout the world. (This organization became a reality in 1919, with the formation of the League of Nations.) Although the United States' military contribution to the war up to this point had been small, Wilson's speech made a great diplomatic contribution.

"[Admiral Sims] influenced our naval course more than any man who ever wore the uniform."

The New York Herald Tribune, after the death of Admiral William Sims in 1936

"It must be a peace without victory. . . . Only a peace between equals can last."

President Wilson, 1917

The League Leads to the United Nations

President Wilson may not have been aware of it at the time, but his famous "Fourteen Points" speech made a dramatic impact on the future of the world. In the last of his points, he spoke of establishing an organization to promote cooperation among nations around the world. This world peacekeeping body would be the League of Nations.

The United States did not become a member due to opposition in Congress, but many other nations did join the League of Nations. In the 1930s, the League of Nations suffered setbacks and was ineffective as a tool to avoid World War II. However, the League was successful in bringing the world closer to international peace efforts.

During World War II, President Franklin Delano Roosevelt built on the ideals that Wilson had set forth by taking steps to create a worldwide peacekeeping body that would help prevent future conflicts. After Roosevelt's death, President Harry S. Truman carried on that same work. On January 1, 1942, a "Declaration by United Nations" was made by 26 countries. Over the next three years, these countries discussed the formation of the United Nations (UN).

Delegates from 50 nations met in San Francisco, California, in April 1945 to create a charter for the UN. It was signed on June 26 and went into effect on October 24, 1945.

The United Nations now has about 190 nations in its membership. They all take part in meetings of the General Assembly, which decides overall UN policy. In addition to the General Assembly, the 15-member Security Council deals with specific problems and settles international disputes.

5

Americans in the War

The end of the war was in sight and peace negotiations were being discussed, but the fighting continued. In 1918, American soldiers had their first combat experiences on the western front.

Battle at Cantigny

In March 1918, Erich Ludendorff, one of the most important German leaders during the war, led a massive attack on the French and British on the western front. This situation left both the Allies and Paris, the French capital, vulnerable. On March 26, the Supreme War Council responded by appointing French General Ferdinand Foch as supreme commander of Allied forces in Europe. Pershing became more lenient about turning American soldiers over to Allied leaders, telling Foch he could rely on whatever he needed.

A few weeks later, Foch placed the First Division of the U.S. Army near the village of Cantigny, which was on high ground and an important observation point. On May 27, French tanks and 4,000 American troops advanced into the village. It was the Americans' first offensive attack in the war. There were several counterattacks and U.S. casualties numbered 1,607 by the time the battle ended on May 30, but the Americans had gained ground and held their own.

This first American victory in Europe was not a significant military win, but it showed both the Central Powers and the Allies that the "Yanks" knew how to fight. This was especially important because a month earlier, on April 20, German soldiers had staged a surprise attack on

> "... all that we have are yours. Use them as you will."
>
> *General Pershing to General Ferdinand Foch, supreme commander of Allied forces in Europe, March 1918*

General Pershing, (center left) commander of the U.S. forces and General Foch, (center right) commander of all Allied forces on the western front, shake hands at the port of Brest, France, in 1918.

Americans at a training camp, and there had been almost 650 casualties. This early defeat, followed by victory at Cantigny, was just the beginning of the war for the Americans.

Germans Approach the French Capital

The Germans continued to advance, getting ever closer to Paris during their third major offensive of the war. Parisians were fleeing their city in fear. By June 1, 1918, German troops reached the Marne River near Château Thierry, just 56 miles (90 km) from the French capital.

The American victory at Cantigny inspired Foch to call once more for aid from Pershing. The United States Second and Third Divisions were deployed to the Marne River to fill holes in the French line wherever necessary. In a minor battle at Château Thierry, soldiers from the Third Division stopped the Germans in their tracks. A bridge was blown up, keeping the Germans from crossing the Marne. Foch also sent American troops north through the city of Meaux, to fend off Germans creeping closer toward Paris. These victories were critical for bolstering French morale, which was quickly sinking with each major advance made by the German forces.

The Germans continued to maneuver their way toward Paris and advance their bulging front line. Although they had been stopped at Château Thierry, some went a few miles west toward Belleau Wood and others went east toward Jaulgonne, crossing the Marne with long ladders laid across the river. But the Americans were there, capturing about 100 Germans and sending the rest fleeing back across the river. Belleau Wood would be a tougher struggle.

Belleau Wood

On June 6, 1918, a small group of Marines from the Second Division, in addition to soldiers from the Third Division, prepared for their first major AEF battle. Belleau Wood was a small and insignificant patch of forest, but there it became clear to the Germans that the Americans had come to fight. This conflict would last three long weeks, until June 26.

James G. Harbord commanded the soldiers who fought at Belleau Wood. He was later criticized for failing to lead the fight efficiently. At first, the German artillery fire was so fierce that, in one push, 380 out of 400 American lives were lost. But slowly, the Americans fought back and gained ground. In the end, Belleau Wood fell to the Americans, but not without severe losses. In all, over 7,000 American soldiers were wounded and hundreds killed.

It was a significant victory for the Allies. Many French divisions had become exhausted by the war, but the U.S. win again showed the Central Powers that the AEF posed a significant threat. A German commander at Belleau Wood said the American outfit "must be considered a very good one and may even perhaps be reckoned as a storm troop."

In their offensive during the spring months of 1918, the Germans launched attacks on newly arrived U.S. troops in France. These American soldiers were advancing into a German attack of mustard gas in May 1918. The soldier on the left was overcome by the poisonous gas when his gas mask failed to protect him.

Soldiers of the 93rd Division fighting in the trenches during World War I.

African American Soldiers

When World War I began, America was still very much a segregated nation. The same was true of the United States Army. Blacks and whites did not serve together, and most of the 400,000 African Americans in the military were assigned to labor duties such as cooking and cleaning.

During World War I, however, about 40,000 African American men fought for their country. There were two main African American divisions of infantry (soldiers who fight on foot) stationed in France. One of them, the 92nd Division, suffered from a lack of decent training and low morale because its white commanders were prejudiced against blacks. Unfortunately, this furthered the mistaken idea that African American men did not make good soldiers.

However, the 93rd Division did much to prove that notion wrong. Two of its regiments were awarded honors for excellence in the Meuse-Argonne offensive in 1918. In a different battle, another regiment captured 1,900 Germans in one day. And a fourth regiment fought alongside one of the fiercest French units, showing beyond a shadow of a doubt that they were excellent soldiers. In all, more than 500 African American soldiers in the 93rd Division received French medals for bravery.

While the French treated the black soldiers as equals, many white American soldiers harassed them. Some AEF officers were annoyed that the black soldiers had been honored, and assigned them the terrible duty of looking for bodies and burying slain servicemen. But when the 369th regiment of the 93rd Division arrived in New York after the war's end, they were welcomed with a homecoming parade and a cheering crowd of nearly a million people.

Second Battle of the Marne

By June 1918, there were 25 U.S. divisions in France that Pershing could make available to Foch, who was about to need more reinforcements. While the battle at Belleau Wood was being waged, Ludendorff became more determined than ever to defeat the French. He launched yet another German offensive on June 9. The Germans were held off by French and American soldiers.

Ludendorff then needed to decide whether to concentrate efforts against British or French targets, since he had limited resources left to bring the war to conclusion. He chose the French, and lunged again on July 15 in the Second Battle of the Marne at the Marne River. (The First Battle of the Marne had taken place in September 1914.) This time, nine U.S. divisions were put under Foch's command. French, British, and Italian troops also fought in this battle. For three days, the Allies kept the Germans from gaining. On July 18, Foch made his move at Soissons. With tanks and soldiers, the Allies streamed through the German line. By noon, the German front near Soissons was broken.

The Second Battle of the Marne marked a turning point in the war. From that point on, the German army steadily retreated and lost its advantage. However, this was also the first battle in which the United States suffered severe casualties: Of the 85,000 American troops who took part, about 30,000 were killed or wounded.

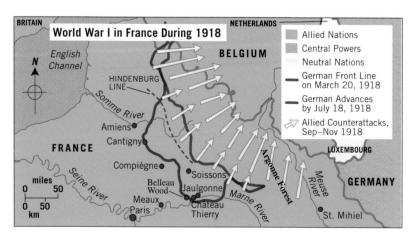

By the summer of 1918, American forces in Europe were trained and up to strength. They contributed significantly in the fight against the Germans. The Allies started their final offensive in September, and succeeded in steadily pushing back the German front line.

On August 8, British and French tanks supported by Canadian and Australian troops successfully pushed back the Germans at a critical point near Amiens on the Somme River. During the next few weeks, the Germans would lose all the territory they had gained since the spring.

Battle at St. Mihiel

Up to this point in the war, the Americans had been used to reinforce French and British troops. But on August 30, 1918, Pershing established the independent First American Army. And by the middle of September, his forces were poised for a victory against German troops. The Germans had held the town of St. Mihiel since 1914. Pershing deployed his men there on September 12, launching the first all-American offensive of World War I. The ground offensive was backed by nearly 1,500 planes, the largest Allied air force to date. It was made up of American, French, Italian, Belgian, Brazilian, and Portuguese planes, all under the command of American Colonel Billy Mitchell.

In just a few days during September 1918, the French town of St. Mihiel was battered by Allied airplanes and a huge American ground attack. German soldiers captured in the battle are seen marching on their way to a prison camp behind the American lines.

William Lendrum "Billy" Mitchell (1879–1936)

One of the strongest personalities to emerge during the war was Colonel Billy Mitchell. Born in France, Mitchell was the son of a U.S. senator. He spent his childhood in Milwaukee, Wisconsin, and attended what is now George Washington University in Washington, D.C.

Mitchell enlisted to serve in the Spanish–American War in 1898. In 1901, he set up a military communications system in the wilds of Alaska. Mitchell advanced by leaps and bounds in the army, and by June 1917 was an aviation officer in the AEF. He had the distinction of being the first American pilot to fly over enemy territory. Mitchell was put in command of all Allied air services in 1918. His most outstanding achievement during World War I was the large and successful bombing of St. Mihiel. Mitchell's strategies were also critical during the fighting in the Meuse-Argonne.

After the war, Mitchell was determined to convince the government that an independent air force, separate from the army and navy, was crucial to the military strength of the United States. Twice he tried to make his message heard by blowing up old warships using aircraft. His aggressive methods got him court-martialed in 1926, but Mitchell continued his fight, warning that America was vulnerable without an air force. After his death, many of Mitchell's predictions were realized, including the Japanese air attack on Pearl Harbor in 1941. In 1947, the U.S. Air Force was established.

Aided by the element of surprise, more than 500,000 U.S. troops backed by French artillery defeated the Germans at St. Mihiel and captured more than 15,000 prisoners. One surrender was so large—300 German soldiers led by one American with an empty pistol—that it was almost mistaken as a German counterattack. However, the victory of the First American Army was not without loss. More than 1,000 Americans were killed at St. Mihiel and 5,000 wounded.

The Allies Win the War

World War I extended far beyond the western front. The war had been waged in the Balkans, the Middle East, the Italian Alps, and as far as Africa. Throughout much of the war,

Austria-Hungary, the Ottoman Empire, and Bulgaria relied on Germany for reinforcements. Even by late 1917, the Central Powers were struggling. And by July 1918, the reliable German forces were weakening. The eastern front began to crumble.

Allied soldiers beat the Bulgarian army and that nation surrendered on September 30, 1918. The British defeated the Ottoman army in the region of Palestine and what is now the nation of Syria, and the Ottoman Empire signed an armistice on October 30. The Italians defeated Austria's last effort in the battle of Vittorio Veneto at the end of October, and Austria-Hungary requested an armistice. The Allies regained Belgrade, the Serbian capital, on November 1. As the end of 1918 approached, Germany stood alone.

Back on the western front, the British broke through the critical German Hindenburg Line of defense (see map on page 51) at the end of September 1918. Following St. Mihiel, heavy fighting occurred in the region between the Argonne Forest and the Meuse River. The British were pushing back the Germans at the Belgian border. The Germans did not

American soldiers of the Sixth Infantry Regiment in France celebrate the end of World War I in November 1918. More than 112,000 members of the U.S. armed forces had died during the war, over half of them in pneumonia and influenza epidemics that swept through their camps. Nearly 49,000 died in battle and 230,000 were wounded.

lose substantial ground but were nevertheless overwhelmed.
It was clear that the war was coming to an end.

On November 3, 1918, members of the German navy
rebelled against their commanders. Food shortages had
weakened the reserves of German sailors, soldiers, and
civilians, and a worldwide epidemic of influenza was taking
the lives of thousands of people. There were riots against
the German ruler, Kaiser Wilhelm, in some German cities.
The kaiser fled and Ludendorff was forced to resign.

In 1918, at the eleventh hour on the eleventh day of
the eleventh month, the war was officially over. Germany
accepted the terms of the Allied armistice and it was signed
aboard a train in the French forest of Compiègne.

The Treaty of Versailles and the League of Nations

In January 1919, the Allied leaders met in Paris to establish
terms for peace. Representatives included British Prime
Minister Lloyd George, French Premier Georges Clemenceau,
Italian Premier Vittorio Orlando, and U.S. President Wilson.
The smaller Allied nations were included mainly as observers
and the Central Powers were not invited to contribute.

The conference was intended to be a calm gathering
focused on creating peaceful relationships and patching up
the war-torn world. Instead, it escalated into squabbles and
disagreements. Some of the items in Wilson's Fourteen Points
had already been achieved. But Wilson was determined to
persuade the other leaders to stick to his entire plan and
they became annoyed. Amidst a general lack of cooperation,
Orlando, Clemenceau, and Lloyd George argued over
territorial gains.

In the end, the Allies (but not the United States) and a
reluctant Germany signed the Treaty of Versailles on June 28,
1919. It was five years to the day since the Archduke Franz
Ferdinand had been killed. The remaining Central Powers
later signed separate treaties, and these treaties together
were called the Peace of Paris. Germany was made to accept

"God gave us His
Ten Commandments,
and we broke them.
Wilson gave us his
Fourteen Points—
we shall see."

*Premier Clemenceau
of France, December
1918*

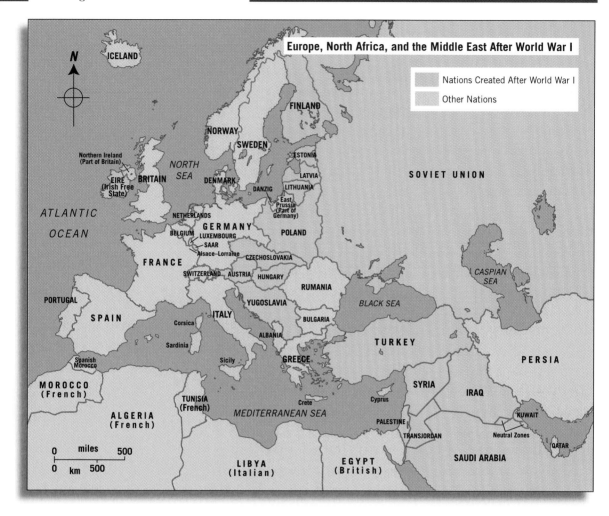

Europe, North Africa, and the Middle East After World War I

Nations Created After World War I

Other Nations

A new Europe was created after World War I by the Treaty of Versailles. Germany was forced to give up territory, causing a simmering resentment in that country that would have serious results in the future. New nations were formed as the Austro-Hungarian and Ottoman Empires were dissolved.

full responsibility for the war, and to pay the Allies for damages and losses. (The sum of $56 billion was not set until 1921.) In addition, the German army and navy were both reduced.

The treaty dramatically affected national boundaries, and the map of Europe was redrawn. The Austro-Hungarian Empire was broken apart and the new nations of Yugoslavia and Czechoslovakia emerged. Other new, independent nations were also created, including Poland, Estonia, Latvia, Lithuania, and Finland. Germany had to return Alsace-Lorraine to France and give up overseas territory. German land west of the Rhine River went to the Allies.

The Treaty of Versailles also established the League of Nations. The United States refused to enter into either the Treaty of Versailles or the League. An influential senator from Massachusetts, Henry Cabot Lodge, led the opposition, saying America had to put its own interests first. He believed in isolationism, which is when a country refuses to enter into military alliances or political treaties with other nations. The war was over, and Senator Lodge's belief reflected the opinion of many Americans.

The Repercussions of War

Although the end of World War I brought relief, the ideal of fighting for democracy had not matched the reality of war. The belief that advanced technology would lead to a swifter war with fewer casualties was shattered. Instead, more lives had been lost in new and brutal ways.

The financial strain of World War I strengthened the notion among Americans that their nation should stay out of conflicts abroad. Americans entered a renewed period of isolationism as the majority observed that the overall cost of war was too high. This feeling against other nations extended to immigrants, and legislation restricting immigration to the United States was soon passed. The overall feeling about involvement in foreign affairs was "never again." Of course, it would happen again: World War II was not far off.

Important changes took place in Europe as a result of World War I, as empires crumbled and independent republics grew. Russia under Lenin was no longer peaceful. And by the end of the 1920s, democracy throughout Europe would become threatened.

Germany especially, would rise from its defeat with a vengeance. The blame placed on Germany for World War I angered Adolf Hitler, the man who would become the German leader. Hitler felt the Versailles Treaty was unfair on Germany, and this was one motive for his attempt to dominate Europe. After World War I, he succeeded in rousing the German people to avenge their humiliation with aggression toward other nations. This led, in 1939, to World War II. In this regard, therefore, World War I had not lessened the likelihood of a second total war, but had contributed to it.

6

The Nation Regroups

Although America was an industrial power before the war, the nation was not a leading force in the world's economy. World War I, however, turned the United States into one of the leading global powers.

A Creditor Nation

America became a creditor nation, meaning that other countries owed the United States large sums of money. Britain and France had needed huge amounts of American supplies during World War I. Also, the Allies had borrowed large amounts of money to pay for their war efforts. In fact, between Britain and France, $10 billion was owed to the United States. However, due to problems in the European postwar economy, this was not money that the United States could count on receiving in the immediate future. In addition, the U.S. government and American companies had invested in factories and railroads overseas, businesses that were now struggling.

After the war, Britain and France continued to rely on American goods and imported mass quantities from the United States. In contrast, there was little being produced in postwar Europe. This situation put the United States in a powerful position.

Postwar Unrest

Despite the celebration of war's end in the United States, a certain amount of unrest developed. Factories that had been converted for the production of war materials had to be transformed for a second time in order to return to the production of consumer goods. There were other problems, such as providing enough jobs for returning soldiers and upholding the rights of working people.

Workers had been struggling for change in their working conditions for several years, with increasingly violent outcomes. Strikes were held, mainly to protest layoffs or salary cuts, and this union activity worried some people. They were afraid of the sort of communist revolution that had brought Lenin to power in Russia.

In 1919, police officers in Boston, Massachusetts, went on strike. Citizens, unprotected by their police force, grew increasingly nervous. It was a tense and unpredictable time in which isolated and brief incidents of violence occurred. Certain influential people, such as U.S. Attorney General A. Mitchell Palmer, Justice Oliver Wendell Holmes, and businessmen John Rockefeller and J. P. Morgan, were sent bombs in the mail, although many of the devices were detected before they reached their final destinations.

Radicals of any kind became targets in this atmosphere. It didn't take long for the focus of suspicion to move from the Germans, now safely defeated, to people who supported Russian, or "Red," ideas of communism. Palmer led a search for Americans who had joined the Communist party. In a series of raids on Communist party headquarters, nearly 6,000 people were arrested.

Palmer created the General Intelligence Division led by J. Edgar Hoover. Any person thought to be connected to a radical organization or publication was put on a list. Hoover listed about 150,000 people deemed to be un-American.

This was the view Americans had of the creeping threat of communism during the "Red Scare" after World War I. In this cartoon, a Bolshevik is trying to bring his ideas into America, represented by the United States flag. Bolshevism is an extreme form of communism, and its followers believe in the violent overthrow of non-communist governments.

The Great Migration

The changing makeup of America's cities also affected the atmosphere of the nation. Huge numbers of blacks from the South migrated to the North in search of jobs, education, and freedom from fear and prejudice. They hoped for better treatment in Northern society. Between 1916 and 1920, half a million African Americans moved from Southern states to Northern ones. New York, Chicago, Philadelphia, and Boston all had growing black neighborhoods that attracted those who fled the South. And as the numbers grew in the cities, large, predominantly black communities such as Chicago's South Side and New York's Harlem were created.

But the North was not free from prejudice either, and soon its own racial tension increased as a result of the changing populations. By the summer of 1919, tempers ran as high as the temperatures in many overcrowded cities where blacks and whites were crammed together. There were race riots in Chicago, Washington, D.C., and other cities that were struggling to adjust to the changes.

In the black urban communities, a new intellectual and cultural life emerged. Many African American writers and

The office of the NAACP's Crisis *journal, shortly after the NAACP was founded. The* Crisis *was edited by W. E. B. Du Bois (standing, right) from 1910 until 1932, and promoted the cause of civil rights for African Americans.*

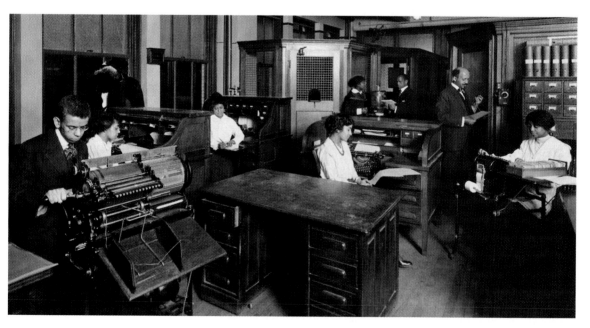

William Edward Burghardt (W. E. B.) Du Bois (1868–1963)

W. E. B. Du Bois was the first African American to receive a doctoral degree from Harvard University. He became professor of history and economics at Atlanta University in 1896. Du Bois was one of the founders of the NAACP and from 1910 to 1933 served as its director of publicity and research. He also edited the NAACP journal, the *Crisis*, until 1932. After another period at Atlanta University as head of the sociology department, he returned to the NAACP in 1944. Throughout his career, Du Bois served in many organizations and arranged conferences to promote advancement for black people.

Du Bois was both brilliant and controversial. He published many academic papers and books about black society and grew to believe that protest and militant action were the only ways to bring about social change. Du Bois believed in equal rights, and thought that force would ultimately be needed to achieve that goal.

In 1961, Du Bois left America to live in Ghana, Africa. He gave up his U.S. citizenship and joined the Communist party.

thinkers were especially attracted to the excitement in the neighborhood of Harlem in New York City. In what became known as the Harlem Renaissance, black poetry, novels, and newspapers found their audiences. And pride in black culture inspired a new interest in African American history, art, and music.

The NAACP and the UNIA

During this time, the National Association for the Advancement of Colored People (NAACP) grew in influence. W. E. B. Du Bois, Ida Tarbell, and others had founded the organization in 1909. It remained small until the black northward migration helped to bring African American issues to the nation's attention. The NAACP set out to secure equal rights for African Americans and pass laws prohibiting racial violence.

> "The Negro must have a country, and a nation of his own."
>
> *Marcus Garvey, 1924*

Members of the Ku Klux Klan dressed in white cloaks and hoods, a costume they had adopted in the late 1800s to frighten blacks into thinking they were ghosts of the Civil War dead. The Klan operated at night, going out on raids or performing ceremonies such as this one in 1915, where new members were initiated.

Other voices also spoke out for black rights. One notable figure was Marcus Garvey, who had a very different approach from the NAACP. Instead of urging white Americans to accept blacks as equals, Garvey wanted blacks to celebrate their African heritage, supported a return to Africa, and encouraged a separate black society within America. His organization, founded in 1920, was called the Universal Negro Improvement Association (UNIA). Garvey's newspaper, the *Negro World*, was read throughout the United States and overseas.

The Ku Klux Klan Revival

The rapid growth of cities and the challenges brought by growth also triggered the return of one organization dedicated to intolerance. The Ku Klux Klan (KKK) was a secret society, and its members appeared in public shrouded in white robes and hoods. They were dedicated to keeping white, Protestant people supreme in American society.

The KKK had its roots in the Reconstruction period of the 1860s and 1870s, but had faded into near nonexistence. In 1915, it was revived in Georgia, and by the mid-1920s more than 4 million people belonged to the Klan. The Communist Revolution in Russia and the migration of blacks to the North played a big part in the renewed growth of the KKK.

The Klan did not, however, devote all of their hatred to blacks and communists. They also targeted Jewish people, Catholics, immigrants, and what they believed was the sinful atmosphere of the cities. Their tactics were often violent and bloody.

The organization's power grew during the early 1920s. Some Klan members entered politics, while others succeeded in influencing politicians who were not in the KKK. In some cases, this was done with fear and intimidation. In other instances, shared philosophies of intolerance were the cause. By 1928, however, public opinion turned against the Klan's terrible activities, and membership dropped off dramatically.

Women Win the Right to Vote

Before 1920, American women were not allowed to vote in national elections. In 1910, there was an increase in the number of suffragettes, women who fought to gain the right to vote. Rallies and parades were held all over the country for the next decade. At one lengthy march in Washington, D.C., a large banner was carried that read, "20 Million American Women Are Not Self-Governed." There was a strong and growing sense of unity in the suffrage movement.

During World War I, women in America continued to fight for the right to vote, and the war itself affected their cause. Nearly 1.5 million women had entered the workforce by 1918 to fill jobs left vacant by men in the armed forces. In addition to this, women were doing jobs that would have been unthinkable a few years earlier. Women worked on assembly lines, in construction, and making weapons. Because of the war, there were suddenly many opportunities for women to prove themselves equal to men.

"By keeping women out of politics, the soul of our country is diminished by one-half."

National Woman Suffrage Association

Carrie Chapman Catt was one of the most important suffragettes. She took over the presidency of the National American Woman Suffrage Association (NAWSA) in 1900 and gave the organization new life. Catt's strategies played a major role in securing the vote for women, and by 1918 President Wilson had been persuaded to support the cause. On August 26, 1920, years of struggle, dedication, and hard work by American women paid off. The Nineteenth Amendment was passed and all adult women at last had the right to vote.

Harding Becomes President

In the 1920 election, the Republican candidate Warren Harding was swept into office. He captured more than 61 percent of the vote, soundly beating the Democratic candidate James Cox.

Carrie Chapman Catt (1859–1947)

Carrie Clinton Lane grew up in the Midwest and became a schoolteacher. In 1883, she was appointed one of the nation's first female superintendents of schools. She was married twice, to Leo Chapman in 1885 and, after Chapman's death, to George Catt in 1890.

Catt worked for the Iowa Woman Suffrage Association from 1887 to 1892. During her time there, she rose within the organization to become its leader. Catt then became president of the National American Woman Suffrage Association (NAWSA) from 1900 to 1904. During that period, she helped establish the International Woman Suffrage Alliance (IWSA) and later spent several years working overseas as its president.

In 1915, Catt again took over NAWSA. Her work there helped bring about the Nineteenth Amendment in 1920, which gave the vote to all American women. In 1919, Catt established the League of Women Voters to promote voter education for women. She remained its honorary president until she died. Catt's accomplishments in advancing women's rights were enormous, and in later years she added to her achievements by working for world peace and against child labor.

Carrie Chapman Catt takes part in one of many parades held in American cities during the 1910s to promote women's right to vote. Catt was a leader of the suffrage movement in the early 1900s, and it is largely due to her efforts that American women were given the vote in 1920.

Harding himself was unsure of his qualifications to run the nation. His strategy was to surround himself with the best advisers. He chose a former Supreme Court Justice, Charles Evans Hughes, as secretary of state. Hughes strengthened the nation's position on foreign affairs by organizing international conferences and treaties. Another clever move by Harding was to appoint Herbert Hoover as secretary of commerce.

The president made a bad mistake, though, when he chose Albert B. Fall for secretary of the interior. During Wilson's administration, Congress had set aside oil-rich lands in Wyoming for the U.S. Navy. In 1922, Fall secretly leased

Warren Harding (1865–1923)

Warren Gamaliel Harding was born in Ohio. He was the oldest of eight children and grew up working on the family farm. He went to Ohio Central College when he was 14. In 1884, when he was only 19, Harding bought an Ohio newspaper that was going out of business, the Marion *Star*, and became its publisher.

Harding's wife, whom he married in 1891, encouraged him to go into politics, and Harding joined the Ohio state senate in 1900. In 1904, he became lieutenant governor of Ohio, and in 1914 won a seat in the U.S. Senate. Attractive, charming, and pleasant to be around, the senator became very popular.

When the Republican party needed to nominate a president for the 1920 election, Harding was chosen because he took neither side in a debate about whether Republicans should support the League of Nations. The American people, tired of the rigid and serious President Wilson, saw Harding as a welcome change. He beat the Democratic candidate easily. After a fairly ineffective presidency, Harding died suddenly on August 2, 1923, before the end of his first term.

this land, called the Teapot Dome Oil Reserve, to a private oil company. He did the same thing with government-reserved oil fields in Elk Hills, California. Making matters even worse, Fall personally received the sum of $25,000 from the Wyoming transaction and another $100,000 in the California deal. In addition to appointing Fall, Harding had also placed Charles Forbes, a close friend, at the head of the Veterans' Bureau, where Forbes misused funds.

Fall's and Forbes' dishonesty was not uncovered until later, but persistent rumors of corruption affected Harding's presidency, although he was innocent himself. When the dishonest deals did come to light in 1924, after Harding's death, several government officials, including Fall and Forbes, were sentenced on charges of fraud and bribery. Together, the collective scandals associated with the Harding administration are called the "Teapot Dome Affairs."

Tomb of the Unknowns

There is no monument in the United States that specifically honors the Americans who did not return home from World War I. The memorials that do exist for them are in Europe, where they lost their lives fighting for democracy and peace. But one U.S. memorial does remind us of their contribution.

The Tomb of the Unknowns in the Arlington National Cemetery, Virginia, honors the memory of soldiers who fought in World War I, World War II, the Korean War, and the Vietnam War. Four unknown American soldiers—one from each of those wars—were buried in the tomb. (In 1998, scientific testing identified the previously unknown Vietnam soldier and his family reburied him elsewhere.)

The white marble memorial is massive, weighing 79 tons (71.7 metric tons). Each year, visitors lay about 3,000 wreaths on the Tomb of the

Unknowns, including one placed by the president on Veterans' Day, November 11. Soldiers guard the tomb 24 hours a day, 365 days a year, performing a ceremony that marks the changing of the guard every hour during the day and every two hours at night. The guards are selected for their excellent physical fitness and behavior. They are required to look straight ahead without talking, smiling, or making any gestures other than performing their duties.

The Roaring Twenties

By 1920, most of the postwar unrest had died down. President Harding's promise for a "return to normalcy" was exactly what the American people wanted. But "normal" wasn't all they wanted: People were rejoicing in their newfound economic prosperity, buying every new gadget and enjoying ever broadening forms of entertainment. Radio, movies, music and dance crazes, and literature all provided exciting outlets for Americans. Still, not everyone shared these feelings, and many were in favor of taming America's wilder side.

Prohibition and Speakeasies

On January 16, 1920, the Eighteenth Amendment became law. The amendment made the manufacture and sale (but not the purchase) of alcoholic drinks, or liquor, illegal. The National Prohibition Act, or the Volstead Act, was adopted to enforce the amendment. Many prohibitionists—those who strongly believed that alcohol should be outlawed—had worked for this day and they were delighted. Among them were reformers who believed that drinking among the poor and immigrant communities needed to be controlled. Little did they know how much havoc Prohibition would cause throughout the decade.

Quite simply, the law did not work. Instead, people were encouraged to find ways around the law. Liquor was smuggled into the United States across the Mexican and Canadian borders, or by boats landing at isolated beaches. People hid liquor flasks in their boots, coats, pockets, and other places.

The nation felt newly freed from constraint, and people were not about to let the government dictate how they handled their personal lives.

As saloons across the country were closed, illegal speakeasies sprang up in their places. These new bars took their name from the fact that people had to "speak easy" so police outside would not hear them. The atmosphere of the speakeasy drew out a new variety of drinkers at night. Before Prohibition, bars were frequented mostly by working-class men. But speakeasies attracted women, college students, and professionals as run-down bars were replaced with stylish places filled with great music, a wide choice of drinks, and excitement. Speakeasies became the center of the social scene. They provided a booming business opportunity that produced many colorful personalities. One owner, a lively woman named Texas Guinan, ran so many bars that when one location was raided by the police, she simply moved on to the next.

More than 1,500 federal agents were assigned to enforce Prohibition, a task that would prove impossible because of the sheer number of smugglers and speakeasies involved. And some politicians and police were corrupted in the process, taking money to look the other way.

> "When I sell liquor it's bootlegging. When my patrons serve it on a silver tray on Lake Shore Drive, it's hospitality."
>
> *Gangster Al Capone during Prohibition*

This picture of gang leader Al Capone was taken in a police station in May 1929, when he was arrested some months after the St. Valentine's Day Massacre. Although everyone knew he was responsible, Capone was never convicted for the murders. He was eventually sent to jail, but it was for failing to pay taxes.

The Gangster Era

Prohibition and crime went hand in hand as bootlegging (the illegal manufacturing and selling of liquor) was taken over by gangsters. There had always been gangsters, but bigger and more violent gangs were formed in this period. Systems for brewing, distilling, and transportation were set up. Force was used both to put small bootleggers out of business and to make speakeasy owners purchase alcohol from the new, larger organizations.

There were major gang operations in cities such as Philadelphia, Detroit, and New York.

But the largest, most frightening gang emerged in Chicago. By 1925, Al Capone was the number one gangster in the city. He wore flashy suits, drove a bulletproof Cadillac car specially made by General Motors, and controlled politicians. He became famous as his face and deeds filled the newspapers.

Few people who got in Capone's way survived to tell about it, and he was not the only thug to deal with conflict in a violent manner. Estimates put gang-related murders in Chicago during the 1920s at 500. The worst incident was the St. Valentine's Day Massacre in which, on February 14, 1929, Capone targeted a rival named Bugs Moran. Five of Capone's men ambushed six of Moran's men and gunned them down, along with an innocent bystander. The murderers were never brought to justice.

Entertainment for the Masses

The exciting social life that evolved around drinking during the 1920s was, however, not everyone's favorite pastime. There were plenty of other things to do, and one of the most popular forms of mass entertainment was the radio. The

This kind of radio set was common in family homes by 1929, when this photograph was taken. Before the days of television, children listened to serial stories on the radio. Programs such as "Amos 'n' Andy," "Roxy and His Gang," and "The Lone Ranger" were all favorites by 1930.

The Sports Legends

Attendance at a variety of sports events climbed dramatically during the 1920s. People went in droves to watch baseball, football, and basketball. They followed horse races, boxing, wrestling, and tennis with a new enthusiasm. During this sports craze, legends were born.

George Herman "Babe" Ruth.

George Herman "Babe" Ruth started out as a pitcher with the Boston Red Sox. He joined the New York Yankees in 1920 and became one of the biggest stars baseball has ever known. Babe hit 60 home runs in the 1927 season, a record that would take more than 30 years to break. His winning personality, coupled with his talent as a hitter, brought thousands of fans to the ballparks. When the Yankee Stadium was built in 1923, it was nicknamed "the house that Ruth built" because of all the money in ticket sales generated by his talent.

Harold "Red" Grange, the most famous of the college football players, was called the "Galloping Ghost of Illinois." From 1923 to 1925, while playing for the University of Illinois, Red scored 31 touchdowns. In one game, he scored four touchdowns in the first 12 minutes. After college, Red Grange played professionally and became a millionaire.

Jack Dempsey was the heavyweight boxing champion of the world in 1919. In 1921, his fight against Georges Carpentier marked the first time that an audience had collectively spent more than $1 million to watch boxing. After winning the world championship three times, Dempsey was defeated by Gene Tunney in 1926.

William Tilden and Helen Wills were the first stars of tennis. During the 1920s, "Big Bill" Tilden won the United States men's championship seven times. In 1923, Helen Wills, at the age of 17, captured her first national title and held it through five more championships that decade.

71

technology of radio was not new at the time, but using it for public broadcasts was. In November 1920, the first public radio station, KDKA in Pittsburgh, sent the results of the presidential election over the airwaves. The concept quickly caught on. Within two years there were 500 radio stations.

At first, there were no advertisements but that quickly changed. The first commercially sponsored program aired on August 28, 1922, paving the way for the flood of commercials heard on the radio today. News, church services, and music were broadcast from coast to coast. The first major sports event to be broadcast on the radio was the 1921 boxing match between Jack Dempsey and Georges Carpentier.

The mass production of radios began in 1920 as people clamored for this new source of free entertainment. By 1929, there were 12 million households with radios.

This cover of Smart Set *magazine from 1922 sums up the spirit of the 1920s. Flappers, jazz bands, and the stories of F. Scott Fitzgerald were all part of the "Jazz Age."*

JUNE, 1922   35

The
SMART SET

Edited by
George Jean Nathan
and
H.L. Mencken.

"The Diamond as Big as the Ritz"
By F. Scott Fitzgerald

Magazines and Books

Magazines such as *National Geographic* and *Ladies' Home Journal* were already popular when the 1920s began. And throughout the decade, many new magazines were launched that are still widely read today.

Reader's Digest began in February 1922. It had no advertisements and started with only 1,500 buyers. Within ten years, that number rose to 500,000. *Vanity Fair* catered to a glamorous and sophisticated crowd and was first to print the term "flapper" in May 1922. A flapper was a daring young girl with short hair who dressed in short skirts and wore rolled stockings.

Time magazine hit the stands in March 1923. It recycled news stories from *The New York Times* newspaper and was known for coining new words, adding to the style of the publication. By 1926, *Time* had steady subscribers and was making money. In February 1925, the *New Yorker* went on sale, and wittily portrayed the current times in America.

Some of America's greatest writers brought out new books during the 1920s. The thoughts, characters, and political messages of F. Scott Fitzgerald, Sinclair Lewis, John Dos Passos, Edna St. Vincent Millay, Langston Hughes, Eugene O'Neill, Ernest Hemingway, and many others captured the period. Fitzgerald's works may even be credited with creating as well as reflecting the atmosphere of the period. Dozens of his short stories appeared in magazines and two books in particular, *This Side of Paradise* and *The Great Gatsby*, made him a literary star. Both books portrayed reckless, excessive characters that attracted young readers. Fitzgerald and his wife Zelda personified the times and were famous for living in much the same way as his fictional creations.

> "The uncertainties of 1919 were over. America was going on the greatest . . . spree in history."
>
> *F. Scott Fitzgerald*

Langston Hughes (1902–67)

Langston Hughes was one of the writers who made their mark during the Harlem Renaissance. Born in Missouri, Hughes began writing poetry in high school. He later taught English in Mexico, attended Columbia University for one year, and traveled to Africa and Europe. He then moved to Harlem and became part of the growing black intellectual movement.

In 1921, the NAACP published Hughes' poem "The Negro Speaks of Rivers." His first book of poetry, *The Weary Blues*, was published in 1926. Hughes had a talent and passion for writing about the everyday life of African Americans. Although Hughes was known for his poetry, he wrote acclaimed plays, short stories, and novels as well. He was also a columnist for a black newspaper in Chicago, the *Defender*.

In the 1930s, Hughes helped found several theater companies. He continued to publish his writings throughout his life, and has more than 40 books to his name. Hughes left an important legacy to African Americans in a body of work that paid tribute to black people.

Commenting on a different slice of American life, Sinclair Lewis made a name for himself with his 1920 novel *Main Street*, followed by *Babbitt* and *Arrowsmith*. Lewis turned his biting and critical style on what he saw as the shallowness and intolerance of small-town life in America.

Movie Milestones

In this new age of celebrity, movies drew crowds on a regular basis. Westerns, comedies, gangster movies, and love stories were popular. America now had a kind of cinema "royalty," with such stars as Mary Pickford, Douglas Fairbanks, Rudolph Valentino, Clara Bow, and Greta Garbo. At the beginning of the 1920s, estimated weekly audiences at the movies numbered 40 million. By the end of the decade, that number had climbed to 110 million.

Larger-than-life epic films appeared, such as Cecil B. De Mille's *The Ten Commandments* released in 1923. On October 6, 1927, *The Jazz Singer* opened, starring Al Jolson. It was the first motion picture to match picture and sound. On the lighter side, Charlie Chaplin, Buster Keaton, and Stan Laurel and Oliver Hardy made the masses laugh with their comic styles. Walt Disney brought the cartoon to Hollywood in 1924, and in 1928 he released *Steamboat Willie*, the first cartoon with sound. This movie also brought Mickey Mouse to the screen for the first time.

The movie industry exploded into big business. Hollywood, in

The Kid was released in movie theaters in 1921 and became an instant hit. Starring, written by, and directed by Charlie Chaplin, one of America's favorite comedians, the movie also introduced Jackie Coogan, a child star of the 1920s.

This is the great picture upon which the famous comedian has worked a whole year.

6 reels of Joy.

Charles Chaplin IN "THE KID"

Written and directed by Charles Chaplin

A First National Attraction

large part influenced by Cecil B. De Mille, began to set fashion trends. On March 16, 1924, the massive MGM studio was formed when Metro Pictures, Goldwyn Pictures, and Louis B. Mayer's company merged into MGM.

Dance Crazes

During the 1920s, dancing grew as a popular means of expression. Women, who had previously been constrained by what was deemed "proper," learned new and uninhibited dances. At parties and in nightclubs, dancing became the main attraction.

Flappers were an important part of the dance scene. They knew every step to every new dance, and dressed the part in their short skirts and long, swinging beads. It was a dance called the Charleston, launched in 1924, that made flappers famous and became a symbol of the 1920s. The dance was not easy to learn, but learn it everyone did.

One of the most exhausting fads of the day was the dance marathon. Couples, usually poor people desperate for the prize money, would dance continuously for days on end to see who could last the longest. One Chicago marathon lasted for 119 days. Contestants often suffered fatigue and mental distress, and there were some deaths resulting from heart attacks on the dance floor.

"Of all the crazy competitions ever invented, the dancing marathon wins by a considerable margin of lunacy."

The New York World *newspaper, 1923*

The Jazz Age

The music of the 1920s perhaps set the tone more than any other single thing. Jazz had its origins in the African American culture of New Orleans, but it moved north into New York and Chicago in the early 1920s. A music born out of protest against oppression, jazz was brought to the attention of the nation. White New Yorkers flocked uptown to Harlem to hear it.

In 1920, Joe "King" Oliver's Creole Jazz Band hit Chicago's South Side. Joe Oliver introduced a man who would become a legend: Louis Armstrong. In 1924, Armstrong set off on a solo career and soared to the top. He became one of the most

A young Louis Armstrong (center, in suit and tie) poses with his band in Chicago in 1925. In addition to his horn playing, Armstrong used his voice like an instrument, singing syllables instead of words. This "scat singing" eventually became a standard technique used by vocalists.

"Music must reflect the thoughts and aspirations of the people and the time. My people are American. My time is today."

Composer George Gershwin

influential jazz musicians of all time. Another important figure, Bessie Smith, was dubbed the "Empress of the Blues" because of her beautiful and powerful voice. She toured the South and the Northeast and sold millions of records.

Duke Ellington's unique style of jazz also made him a legend. He became famous at the Hollywood Club in midtown Manhattan and made over 30 records with his band. Ellington and his band opened at Harlem's famous Cotton Club in 1927 and played there until 1931. Many nightclubs offered African American musicians the chance to become successful, changing the face of American music forever. The Cotton Club was the most influential of all.

The music of the Jazz Age greatly affected white musicians and composers, as evidenced by the jazzy feeling of George Gershwin's *Rhapsody in Blue* of 1924. Incredibly, Gershwin wrote almost the entire piece in one week, and improvised many of the piano solos during the performance. During the 1920s, Gershwin also wrote *Piano Concerto in F* and *An American in Paris*. By the time he died in 1937, he was one of the most important American composers.

Miss America

The first Miss America Pageant took place in September 1921, when 16-year-old Margaret Gorman was crowned. The pageant was created to entice tourists to extend their summer stay in Atlantic City, New Jersey. In the first contest, the winner was chosen from eight photographs that were entered. By 1924, there were 83 potential Miss Americas. At the time, the girls represented cities, not states as they do today.

By 1927, the pageant had grown into a week-long event, complete with parades, swimsuit contests, and evening gown competitions. Talent competitions were added in 1935. In 1943, the first college student was crowned. In 1945, the first scholarship money was awarded to the winner, Bess Myerson. The pageant has been televised since 1954, and 30 years later, the first African American Miss America was crowned.

Over the years, the Miss America Pageant has become an American institution. But even in its early days, not everyone cheered the event. Many thought it was degrading to the young women on display and felt the swimsuit competition should be eliminated. That sentiment is still echoed by some Americans today. But one thing is indisputable: The Miss America Scholarship Fund makes more scholarship dollars available exclusively to women than any other fund in the world. And what began as a mere tourist attraction has developed into a strong organization that supports the goals of young American women. As for the pageant, including the controversial swimsuit event, it still causes a stir each September.

Margaret Gorman, the first Miss America.

Innovation
and Politics
in the 1920s

T he 1920s weren't just about having fun. For many, they were also about making money. It was a decade of big business, a booming economy, and new inventions. Milestones included such events as the introduction of a 40-hour working week and the first solo, nonstop, flight across the Atlantic Ocean.

The Automobile Industry

One of the most significant advancements in business at this time was taking place in the automotive industry. Cars were literally changing the face of the American landscape. The earliest paved highways were built, in addition to gas stations, restaurants, and other roadside facilities. The first traffic light was put up in 1922 and the first motel (a combination of the words "motor" and "hotel") was built in 1925. The overall number of cars on America's roads increased from 8 million to 26 million during the 1920s, touching off some of the first traffic jams.

Automobile makers came and went during the birth of this industry, which began before the turn of the century. A handful of them made their mark on history. From the beginning of his career, Henry Ford dreamed of making the greatest number of cars for the lowest prices available to all.

Ford introduced an assembly-line method of production that was a huge success. The system dramatically cut the

"A low wage business is always insecure."

"Every time I lower the price a dollar, we gain a thousand new buyers."

Automobile manufacturer Henry Ford

Henry Ford (1863–1947)

Henry Ford was the oldest of six children and grew up on a farm in Dearborn, Michigan. He left home at 16 to work in Detroit and learn how to be a machinist. When Ford was 28, he was hired as an engineer by the Edison Illuminating Company in Detroit. There, he met Thomas Edison, who encouraged him to pursue his own ideas. Two years later, Ford was promoted to chief engineer. His love of experimenting paid off in 1896, when he invented a self-propelled vehicle with a gas engine called the Quadricycle.

Ford wanted desperately to make automobiles. In 1903, after a considerable amount of hard work, setbacks, and perseverance, the Ford Motor Company was born. It took Ford five years and nine models of cars to figure out how to make one that was affordable and suitable for the average person to drive. The ninth car was the Model T. Ford produced and sold more than 10,000 Model T cars in 1908.

Within a few years, Ford moved to a new factory where he used a moving assembly line to build his vehicles. Ford's techniques skyrocketed him to the top of the industry because he was able to increase production while lowering costs.

Ford possessed certain characteristics that were controversial. He was outspoken on most subjects and felt he knew what was best for most people. Ford also owned a newspaper, the Dearborn *Independent*, that frequently published anti-Jewish articles. Nevertheless, he was a brilliant thinker and his innovations changed people's lives forever.

amount of time it took to make a car and reduced the cost. Ford set a mass production record in May 1921 when his company produced 4,072 cars in one day. That same year, the Ford Motor Company sold close to a million Model T vehicles. In his next move, instead of simply assembling the parts, Ford also created them. He refined iron ore right on the spot to produce iron and steel, and then manufactured the automobile pieces. By 1927, his plant was complete and more than 14 million Model T's had been sold.

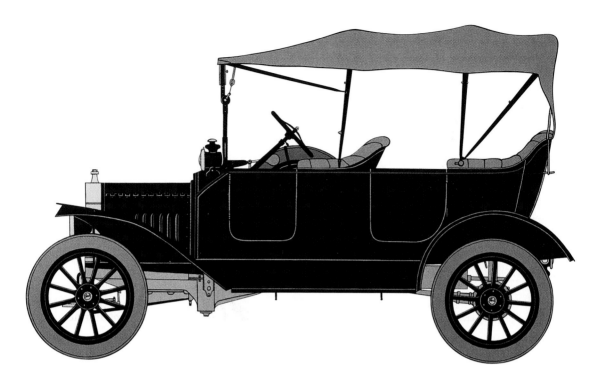

The Model T was first put on the market in 1908 for $850 and sold like wildfire. Within six years, due to his production methods, Ford was able to drop the price to $360. Until 1925, only black Model Ts, such as this touring model from 1915, were available. After that, the Model T was offered in a choice of colors.

Henry Ford was also responsible for improvements in the workplace. He had already set a wage for workers at $5 a day in 1914, a figure that was much higher than the national average. And in September 1926, Ford implemented the first 40-hour workweek: five days a week, eight hours a day.

Innovations

By 1920, another automobile company, General Motors, had also become an empire. General Motors made flashier, more expensive cars than Ford. But the company developed a way to work around the cost by creating installment plans. People could make a partial payment and then continue making payments over time. This idea was so popular that other companies adopted the same policy. Refrigerators, washing machines, radios, furniture, and all sorts of items began to be paid for in installments. The plan that General Motors had instituted was the beginning of buying things on credit.

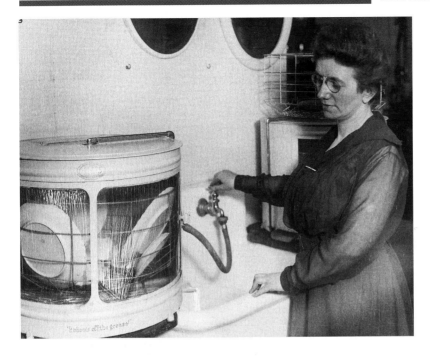

In the 1920s, domestic life was transformed by new gadgets designed to make household tasks easier. Appliances that are now commonplace were new and exciting then, such as this odd-looking dishwasher being demonstrated in 1921.

The 1920s saw many other innovations. In May 1922, a teenager named George Frost used his imagination and a wireless radio to come up with the first car radio. Also related to the popularity of automobiles, the first shopping center opened in Kansas City, Missouri, in 1924. It included parking facilities for more than 5,000 vehicles.

In April 1923, World War I veteran Jacob Schick brought out the first electric shaver. Kleenex introduced disposable tissues in December 1924. In June 1926, the electric pop-up toaster hit the market. And the first air-conditioned office building opened in Texas in February 1928.

Three important firsts were achieved by American pilots in the field of aviation. In August 1922, James Doolittle made the first successful coast-to-coast flight. It took him fewer than 24 hours. The first flight to go all the way around the world, beginning and ending in Seattle, Washington, was completed in 1924.

In 1927, Charles A. Lindbergh found instant fame as the first pilot to make a nonstop, solo, transatlantic flight. A pilot for the Post Office, Lindbergh flew more than 33 hours

On May 20, 1927, Charles Lindbergh stands by his airplane the Spirit of St. Louis *before taking off from the Roosevelt airfield on Long Island, New York. He succeeded in making the first solo flight across the Atlantic, covering 3,600 miles (5,800 km) without stopping.*

without stopping from New York to Paris, France. He was welcomed home with a parade in New York City attended by more than 4 million people.

In the scientific world, astronomer Edward Hubble made the shocking announcement in May 1923 that there were star systems outside of the Milky Way. U.S. physicist Robert Goddard launched the first liquid fuel-propelled rocket in March 1926. And beginning in September 1928, the iron lung, invented by scientist Philip Drinker, was used to help people with respiratory problems to breathe.

Political Changes
When President Harding died on August 2, 1923, Vice President Calvin Coolidge succeeded him as president.

Calvin Coolidge (1872–1933)

John Calvin Coolidge was an only child who grew up on a Vermont farm. Coolidge graduated from Amherst College in Massachusetts in 1895 before studying law. He married Grace Anna Goodhue in 1905 and became mayor of Northampton, Massachusetts, five years later.

Three successful elections followed for Coolidge over the next eight years. He took the offices of Massachusetts state senator, lieutenant governor, and then governor. In 1920, Coolidge was given the Republican nomination for vice president of the United States and took up that post in 1921.

When President Harding died in 1923, Coolidge succeeded him, serving the country until 1929. At the time Calvin Coolidge entered the presidency, his quiet personality was in stark contrast to the exuberant atmosphere of the nation. The United States stayed on a relatively smooth course during the Coolidge administration. The president supported pro-business ideas and handled a few foreign affairs issues. Every day at 12:30 P.M., this shy man shook hands with members of the public inside the Oval Office of the White House. At the end of his presidency, Coolidge told Congress, "The country . . . can anticipate the future with optimism."

He served the remainder of Harding's original term and was reelected in 1924. The Coolidge administration cut taxes and greatly reduced government spending. In addition to this, the international Kellogg-Briand Pact was signed during the Coolidge presidency. In this pact of 1928, the 62 signing nations pledged not to use force against each other to settle their disputes.

In 1929, the Republican Herbert Hoover succeeded Coolidge as president, and Americans welcomed him with enthusiasm. Hoover had a great track record: During World War I, he had organized the Committee for the Relief of Belgium, which managed to get millions of tons of food into Belgium and northern France. Hoover became even more of a hero in the postwar period by providing food relief throughout Europe. As President Harding's secretary of

> "The chief business of America is business."
>
> *President Calvin Coolidge, 1925*

commerce, Hoover also made major improvements in the relationship between the government and big business.

In the first six months of his presidency, Hoover, known as the "Great Engineer," took several important steps. He entertained African Americans in the White House and set up the first White House Conference on Children. Hoover also urged Congress to create a Department of Health, Education, and Welfare.

During his presidential campaign, Hoover had promised to uphold Prohibition and keep the country on a smooth financial course. Unfortunately, before the decade was over he would fail at keeping both promises. Hoover's steadfast embrace of "rugged individualism"—the belief that people should take care of themselves rather than looking to the

Stockbrokers, the people who trade shares for those investing in the stock market, gather around the ticker tape machine, another recent invention. As people rushed to buy and sell shares in the 1920s, the ticker printed out a constant stream of information about the rapidly changing value of stocks.

government to do so—would prove to be his ultimate downfall in the next election.

The Economic Atmosphere

During the 1920s, the gross national product—the total value of goods and services produced by the nation—increased by more than $30 billion. This was due in part to the increased production of new consumer items, such as radios, electric refrigerators, and washing machines. In general, incomes were up and inflation and unemployment were down.

However, the idea that all Americans were either rich or on their way to becoming rich due to the strong economy was just a myth. The truth was that while millions enjoyed their newfound wealth, prosperity had failed to shine upon millions of others. There was an unequal distribution of wealth across the nation.

For example, throughout the farmlands of America, crop prices had dropped and farmers were struggling. A recession in 1920 and 1921 hit farm families especially hard. The economy recovered by 1922, but farmers continued to suffer.

The stock market had become an extremely popular means of making money during the 1920s. People invested their dollars in stocks, which meant they bought shares in a particular company. The basic object of the market is to buy stock in companies at a low price and sell those stocks at a later date for a higher price. The companies that Americans were investing in prospered, and their stock increased in value.

However, as people continued to pour their money into the stock market, the stocks began to be priced much higher than their real value. Stock prices rose at a consistently fast pace toward the end of the decade and Americans bought stock at the same frantic rate. Only a handful of people seemed to be paying attention to the signs that pointed to economic trouble ahead.

The Progress of Flight

On December 17, 1903, the Wright brothers' airplane flew four times in Kitty Hawk, North Carolina. The longest flight lasted 59 seconds and flew over 852 feet (260 m) of land. Over the next five years, the pioneering brothers improved not only their airplane but their flying skills. In August 1908, Wilbur Wright became a hero when he circled above a French racetrack in his plane. In September, Orville Wright flew around an army field in Virginia. The Wright brothers became celebrities. Wilbur knew exactly what they had inspired and afterward said, "The age of flight had come at last."

Very soon, there were airplane factories in both the United States and France. The French government, aware of the possibility of war, helped finance some French factories. By 1914, both the Allies and the Central Powers were using airplanes, changing warfare forever. Planes were used to carry artillery, drop bombs, and scout enemy movements.

After the war, progress was rapid as bigger and better planes were quickly designed. Air races and the setting of new records became popular. The U.S. mail, as well as people, began to be carried by air. By the 1930s, airline companies were forming at a rapid pace.

The airplane continued to be improved and, by World War II, became an even more lethal weapon. The bombs that ended that war could not have been dropped without the bomber planes that were developed. Once jets came along, with no propellers and faster speeds, the airplane industry went hurtling forward. Commercial planes became faster and more efficient, and passenger airlines flourished. Today, millions of people and tons of goods are carried by air every year.

Conclusion

The Progressive Era was a time in which Americans embraced all manner of new ideas and forward thinking. Cities continued to swell with the arrival of both native-born Americans and immigrants, and transportation systems developed at a fast pace. Industrial giants and a new breed of millionaires became richer and more powerful. Yet, at the same time, millions of Americans suffered from poverty.

As the twentieth century began, reforms were taking place to help those that were suffering. The United States was also finding its way as a world power. The long-debated question of whether to remain focused on domestic issues or venture into foreign affairs was always unsettling. But America's ultimate decision to enter World War I put an end to a long period of isolationism.

America was the last to enter the war and suffered the least consequences, although many thousands of Americans died in the conflict. In comparison to the other Allied troops, U.S. soldiers were inexperienced, but they came at a critical time of the war when the Allies were exhausted and morale was sinking. And as victory approached, Wilson's Fourteen Points contributed to the groundwork for peace.

After World War I, the nation celebrated. Incomes were up, unemployment was down, and most Americans seemed to be living the high life. The cities exploded with new kinds of entertainment and money was spent wildly on items from automobiles to company stocks. But in the din of excitement, many overlooked the fact that millions of Americans were not financially stable. A financial crisis was on the horizon that would plunge the United States deep into a state of severe depression.

Glossary

administration The managing of public affairs or business, or the group of people who carry out the management.

alliance An agreement between two or more people, groups, or countries to side together during a conflict. Countries or people with such an agreement become allies.

annexation The act of taking ownership of another nation or adding territory to a nation.

armistice An agreement between parties to stop fighting temporarily.

artillery Large firearms and weapons that fire missiles; and a group of soldiers that uses these weapons.

authority The power to make decisions and rules, or the people who have that power.

commerce The business of buying and selling things.

convoy A protective escort, as in a group of ships sailing together for safety.

corruption Improper conduct that is either dishonest or morally wrong.

democracy Describes a system in which people are their own authority rather than being ruled over by an unelected leader. In a democratic system, people vote on decisions, or elect representatives to vote for them.

diplomacy Negotiations and dealings between nations.

division A large military unit made up of smaller brigades and regiments.

draft A system requiring people by law to serve in the armed forces.

economic To do with the ecomomy, meaning the production and use of goods and services, and the system of money that is used for the flow of goods and services.

environmental To do with the surrounding world, and often used to describe issues concerning the natural world and its protection.

federal To do with the central, or national, government of a country rather than the regional, or state, governments.

front The area of conflict or battle line between opposing armies.

immigrant A person who has left the country of his or her birth and come to live in another country.

inflation A rise in prices due usually to an increase in the amount of money in circulation when there is no similar increase in the amount of available goods and services.

labor union   An organization of workers that exists to improve the working conditions of its members and negotiate on their behalf with employers.

legislation   Laws, or the making of laws.

legislature   An official group of people with the power to make laws, or the branch of government that makes laws.

migration   Movement from one place to another in search of a new place to live.

monopoly   The ownership or control of a particular product or service, or the supply of a particular product or service, by one person or group.

neutral   Not involved in either side of an issue or dispute.

policy   A plan or way of doing things that is decided on, and then used in managing situations, making decisions, or tackling problems.

province   A region of a country, sometimes with its own local administration.

radical   A person who favors distinct political, economic, or social changes or reform.

recession   A time when the economy of a country or region slows down, resulting in businesses cutting back on production and workers losing their jobs.

reform   A change intended to improve conditions.

regiment   A military unit within a division of the armed forces.

segregate   To keep people from different racial or ethnic groups separate, usually with one group having fewer rights than another.

stature   The status or importance developed by a nation or person because of achievements, growth, or increased power.

strategy   The overall plan for dealing with an enemy or a conflict.

tactics   The moves made to try and defeat an enemy.

technology   The knowledge and ability that improves ways of doing practical things. A person performing any task using any tool, from a wooden spoon to the most complicated computer, is applying technology.

treaty   An agreement reached between two or more groups or countries after discussion and negotiation.

veteran   A person who served for a long time at a job, particularly in the military, or who served on a specific campaign or expedition.

Time Line

1886 American Federation of Labor formed.

1887 Dawes Act passed.

1892 Sierra Club founded.

1898 Spanish-American War.
Hawaii annexed by U.S.
Curtis Act passed.

1899 Secretary of State John Hay declares Open Door policy.
American Samoa becomes U.S. territory.

1900 Hawaii becomes U.S. territory.
Boxer Rebellion in China.

1901 President William McKinley assassinated.
Vice President Theodore Roosevelt becomes president.
New Law passed in New York City, creating housing department.

1902 President Roosevelt announces Square Deal.
National Reclamation Act passed.

1903 Wright brothers make historic flight in North Carolina.
Alaska boundary dispute resolved.
United States recognizes Republic of Panama.

1904 Hay-Bunau-Varilla Treaty passed.

1905 Industrial Workers of the World formed.

1906 Antiquities Act passed.
Meat Inspection Act and Pure Food and Drug Act passed.

1907 Oklahoma becomes a state.

1909 William Howard Taft becomes president.
National Association for the Advancement of Colored People founded.

1911 U.S. Supreme Court dissolves Standard Oil.

1912 Alaska becomes U.S. territory.
Arizona and New Mexico become states.

1913 Woodrow Wilson becomes president.
Ford introduces assembly line.
Underwood Tariff Act passed.

1914 Strike begun in 1913 at Colorado Fuel and Iron Company leads to killing of workers and their families.

June 28, 1914	Gavrilo Princip assassinates Archduke Ferdinand.
July 28, 1914	Austria-Hungary declares war on Serbia.
Aug 1, 1914	Germany declares war on Russia.
Aug 3, 1914	Germany declares war on France.
Aug 4, 1914	Germany invades Belgium.
	Britain declares war on Germany.
1915	American Indian Institute founded.
May 1915	Italy joins Allies.
May 7, 1915	Germany sinks the *Lusitania*.
Sept 1915	Bulgaria joins Central Powers.
1916	Wilson reelected president.
	Adamson Act passed.
1917	U.S. purchases Virgin Islands from Denmark.
Feb 1, 1917	Germany renews unrestricted submarine warfare.
April 6, 1917	United States declares war on Germany.
June 26, 1917	First American troops arrive in France.
Nov 9, 1917	Allies form Supreme War Council.
Jan 8, 1918	Wilson delivers "Fourteen Points" speech.
May 27, 1918	Battle of Cantigny begins.
June 6, 1918	Fighting at Belleau Wood begins.
July 15, 1918	Second Battle of the Marne begins.
Sept 12, 1918	Battle of St. Mihiel begins.
Nov 11, 1918	World War I officially ends.
June 28, 1919	Treaty of Versailles signed.
1920	Eighteenth Amendment starts Prohibition.
	Nineteenth Amendment gives vote to women.
1921	Warren Harding becomes president.
1922	First successful coast-to-coast flight by James Doolittle.
1923	Calvin Coolidge becomes president.
1924	Teapot Dome scandals come to light.
1927	First nonstop, transatlantic flight by Charles Lindbergh.
1928	Kellogg-Briand Pact.
1929	Herbert Hoover becomes president.
	St. Valentine's Day Massacre in Chicago.

Further Reading

Blue, Rose and Naden, Corrine. *The Progressive Years: 1901 to 1933.* Austin, TX: Raintree-Steck Vaughn, 1998.

Cooper, Michael L. *Hell Fighters: African American Soldiers in World War I.* New York: Dutton, 1997.

Dolan, Edward F. *America in World War I.* Brookfield, CT: Millbrook Press, 1996.

Haskins, James. *The Harlem Renaissance.* Brookfield, CT: Millbrook Press, 1996.

Jennings, Peter and Brewster, Todd. *The Century: For Young People.* New York: Random House, 1999.

Kent, Zachary. *World War I: "The War to End Wars."* Springfield, NJ: Enslow Publishers, 1994.

King, David. *First Facts About U.S. History.* Woodbridge, CT: Blackbirch Press, 1996.

Meltzer, Milton. *Theodore Roosevelt and His America.* New York: Franklin Watts, 1994.

Uschan, Michael V. *A Multicultural Portrait of World War I.* New York: Benchmark Books, 1995.

Websites

World War I Document Archive – An archive of primary documents from World War I has been assembled by volunteers of the World War I Military History List (WWI-L).
www.lib.byu.edu/~rdh/wwi/

Documents: Women and the Progressive Era – A series of documents that give information re. various women active during the progressive era and the suffrage movement.
www. geocities.com/CollegePark/Campus/6925/doc

Jazz Age Chicago - Main Menu – A close-up look at a major American city during the Jazz Age and its wealth of cultural venues.
www.suba.com/~scottn/explore/mainmenu.htm

Bibliography

Clare, John D., ed. *Living History: First World War*. Orlando, FL: Harcourt Brace & Company, 1995.

Cooper, Michael L. *Hell Fighters: African American Soldiers in World War I*. New York: Dutton, 1997.

The Dawn of the Century: 1900–1910. By the editors of Time-Life Books. Alexandria, VA: Time-Life Books, 1998.

The End of Innocence: 1910–1920. By the editors of Time-Life Books. Alexandria, VA: Time-Life Books, 1998.

Gilbert, Martin. *The First World War: A Complete History*. New York: Henry Holt, 1994.

Gioia, Ted. *The History of Jazz*. New York: Oxford University Press, 1997.

Hakim, Joy. *An Age of Extremes*. New York: Oxford University Press, 1994.

————. *War, Peace, and All That Jazz*. New York: Oxford University Press, 1995.

Heyman, Neil M. *World War I*. Westport, CT: Greenwood Press, 1997.

Hoobler, Dorothy and Thomas. *An Album of World War I*. New York, Franklin Watts, 1976.

The Jazz Age: The 20s. By the editors of Time-Life Books. Alexandria, VA: Time-Life Books, 1998.

Johansen, Bruce E. and Grinde, Donald A. Jr. *The Encyclopedia of Native American Biography*. New York: Da Capo Press, 1997.

Keegan, John. *The First World War*. New York: Knopf, 1999.

MacArthur, Brian, ed. *Twentieth-Century Speeches*. New York: Penguin Books, 1992.

May, Ernest R. *Boom and Bust: 1917–1932*. New York: Time-Life Books, 1974.

————. *The Progressive Era: 1901–1917*. New York: Time-Life Books, 1974.

Perrett, Geoffrey. *America in the Twenties*. New York: Simon and Schuster, 1982.

Stokesbury, James L. *A Short History of World War I*. New York: William and Morrow, 1981.

Weisberger, Bernard A. *Reaching for Empire: 1890–1901*. New York: Time-Life Books, 1975.

Winter, Jay and Baggett, Blaine. *The Great War*. New York: Penguin Studio, 1996.

Index